WORSHIP
IN ANCIENT
ISRAEL

Abingdon Essential Guides

The Bible in English Translation
Steven M. Sheeley and Robert N. Nash, Jr.

Christian Ethics
Robin W. Lovin

Church History
Justo L. González

Feminism and Christianity
Lynn Japinga

Mission
Carlos F. Cardoza-Orlandi

Pastoral Care
John Patton

Preaching
Ronald J. Allen

Rabbinic Literature
Jacob Neusner

WORSHIP
IN ANCIENT
ISRAEL

An
ESSENTIAL GUIDE

Walter Brueggemann

Abingdon Press
Nashville

WORSHIP IN ANCIENT ISRAEL
AN ESSENTIAL GUIDE

This book is printed on acid-free paper.

Library of Congress Cataloging-in-Publication Data

Brueggemann, Walter.
   Worship in ancient Israel : an essential guide / Walter Brueggemann.
     p. cm.
   Includes bibliographical references.
   ISBN 0-687-34336-4 (alk. paper)
   1. Public worship in the Bible.   2. Bible. O.T.—Criticism, interpretation, etc.   I. Title.
   BS1199.P93B78 2005 264—dc22

                      2004027445

05 06 07 08 09 10 11 12 13 14—10 9 8 7 6 5 4 3 2 1
MANUFACTURED IN THE UNITED STATES OF AMERICA

For
Patrick D. Miller

It is the Hebrew intuition that God is capable
of all speech-acts except that of monologue
which has generated our arts of reply,
of questioning and counter-creation.

George Steiner,
Real Presence

Acknowledgments

An attentive reader will notice how much the exposition offered here is informed by and derivative from the work of Patrick Miller. On the one hand, in characterizing the phenomenological dimensions of Israelite worship, I have been informed by Miller's book *The Religion of Ancient Israel*.[1] On the other hand, my consideration of Israel's "normative" practices of worship is greatly illuminated by Miller's book *They Cried To The Lord*.[2] On both counts, I have been stimulated and disciplined by his study. But such a debt to him is simply typical and representative of my immense debts to him over a very long time. On all these counts—and many more—I am glad to dedicate this study to Patrick with thanks and abiding appreciation.

Patrick and I are of course linked more intimately than through our common work. I am glad to acknowledge that Patrick is only one of "the twins," the other being Mary Miller Brueggemann. From her I have learned much about worship, about leadership of worship, and about yielding to the one whom the church worships, Father, Son, and Spirit.

Walter Brueggemann

Contents

CHAPTER 1

Orthodox Yahwism in Dialogic Modes

This book, located in the series that it is, intends to consider some of the leading motifs of ancient Israel's worship traditions in the Old Testament. In addition to being an essential guide to this subject, this book is intended to be in the service of current theological and practical issues concerning the worship of the church in its ecumenical character.

Broadly we may say that worship in the biblical tradition that eventuates in Christian practice consists in regular, ordered, public, disciplined resituation of the life of the community of faith and of each of its members in the presence of the God who has called that community into existence and who continues to call that community into a life of praise and obedience. That regular resituating of one's life and the life of the community is enacted through thick, trustworthy utterances and gestures or, as we say in current ecumenical context, through "word and sacrament." This community has to do, in worship, with the elusive presence and inscrutable purpose of the holy God.[1] For that reason such interaction can only take place in mediated ways through signs that are commonly taken in the community to signify a genuine, direct, and serious

1

relationship. Thus the interaction of God and community through trusted, thick signs constitutes worship. Worship then consists in the faithful management of, practice of, and engagement with these *signs* through which God makes God's self available in defining and decisive ways to this community. This community in turn derives its very life from this God and from God's peculiar and abiding commitment to this community.

The study of worship in the Old Testament is profoundly complex and problematic; for the most part, that study has been understood primarily as a report on the "history of religion," that is, the way in which practices of worship have been ordered and shaped over time in various contexts.[2] Such studies characteristically stop short of articulating the *normative* accents that were surely present in Israel's practice.[3] The study of the history of worship in ancient Israel is crucial because the evidence stretches over long periods and in a variety of different contexts; care must be taken, moreover, that a normative statement concerning worship should not be reductionist of the rich variety of evidence in the text. Given the present state of our knowledge, scholars believe it is possible to trace, in a rough form, the ways in which worship was practiced in various contexts and then was vigorously adjusted and transformed under continuing contextual pressures to take a variety of new shapes. The location of specific worship practices in specific social contexts has made it possible, in a general way, to reconstruct the course of historical development. The classic assumption of Old Testament interpretation, now greatly in dispute, is that Israelite worship developed dramatically from primitive, mythological, and polytheistic forms into more fully monotheistic, ethical, and critically sophisticated worship.[4] That notion of historical development, however, is greatly impinged upon by the more recent recognition of sociological diversity in the community of Israel.[5] As a result it is clear that there was not at any given time in ancient Israel a single practice of worship; rather in every generation and in every social

2

context, there was no doubt a more formal worship practice geared to large truth claims and allied with dominant social power. At the same time, however, alongside that more formal practice there were always "lesser" worship practices connected to "lesser" subcommunities, such as family, clan, or tribe.[6] These several practices more than likely existed in parallel, occasionally overlapped or influenced each other, but characteristically had their own particular interest, nuance, and witness. Thus one must reckon with a pluriform practice upon which no uniformity could be imposed and from which no simplistic practice could emerge.

It is evident that Israel participated in and appropriated from the worship practices of its environment that were very old and well established, for the propensity to worship was in that culture long antecedent to the emergence of Israel. Indeed, that ancient culture, like every culture, was permeated with worship. As Walter Harrelson notes, a hypothesis about secularization in contemporary life should not be overstated:

> What is overlooked [in such secularism] is man's need to celebrate. Human beings, in virtue of their humanity, are evoked to praise by the very process of living their lives. Our response to our work, to our fellow men, to the values and the evils of our time is not a full response unless our lives be centered upon that which must be greeted with praise and upon that which must be greeted with revulsion or the cry of dereliction.... I would insist that man cannot live a fully human life without acts of celebration.[7]

The cultural environment in which Israel emerged offers ample evidence of the need for "acts of celebration." In the ancient world as in the contemporary world, celebration of and encounter with "the transcendent" is an inescapable need. Israel's worship emerged in a cultural environment where that need for celebration and encounter with "the transcendent" was not at all restrained.[8] There were well-established practices and rich resources available to Israel from the outset. While Israel's worship was distinctive in its reference to YHWH, it did not need to reinvent the wheel of worship.

We may identify two aspects of that cultural environment that are important for Israel's worship. First, the great states of the ancient Near East, Egypt and various centers of power in Mesopotamia, developed highly sophisticated mythical accounts of the world that served, at the same time, a theological function in creating a "world" of stability and order, and a political function of legitimating established power.[9] There is no doubt that over time Israel appropriated these great founding narratives for liturgical enactment in ways that featured YHWH as creator God and that identified the Davidic king as human regent for the purposes of the creator God.[10]

Second and more immediately, Israel lived in the sociopolitical context of Canaan, and so inescapably in the midst of Canaanite religion, the character of which we know best from the finds at Ras Shamra (ancient Ugarit).[11] There are biblical texts showing YHWH in deep conflict with Baal, the principle God of Canaanite religion (as in 1 Kgs 18), and there is a strong interpretive tradition of "YHWH versus Baal."[12] It seems clear, nonetheless, that Israel appropriated for its own purposes much of the religious practice and much of the theological understanding of such cultural religion, transposing it only here and there in order to accommodate Yahwistic claims. The antithesis between Canaanite religion and Yahwistic faith has no doubt been overstated in recent scholarship, for it is clear that much of Israel's worship is appropriated and inhaled from that religious environment.[13] And of course, it is not difficult to understand why. Israel appropriated means and forms of worship from its social environment. Just like their Canaanite neighbors, Israelites had to be concerned over the most elemental processes of life and death and over the inscrutable processes of "nature" that governed the destiny of an agricultural community. The commonality of Canaanite religion and Israelite worship applies particularly to the term "fertility" that has been used pejoratively in much recent interpretation, as in "Canaanite fertility religion" against which scholars have been deeply polemical.[14] Such religion found divine presence and divine purpose at work in the normal course of life processes—birth and death—and understood such "natural" processes as permeated with divine power. While such a concern in Canaanite culture produced religious oddities and excesses that offended Yahwists, it is important to recognize, nonetheless, that Israel also worshiped a God linked to context and powerfully engaged in normal processes of life and death. It could not be otherwise in an agricultural economy. Such "syncretistic" or "heterodox" dimensions to Israelite worship only attests that Israel's worship is generated by and sustained by social-sacral practices that function in the real world.[15] From that inescapable reality, we may in our own time and place realize how deeply contextual the church's worship is, even if we imagine and hope for a more "pure version" that reflects disciplined faith and that is not propelled by contextual, cultural pressures.

Given all of the rich diversity and complexity of worship traditions in the Old Testament, and all of the evident development of practice from one context to another, it is nonetheless possible to identify some thematics in the faith and worship in Israel that are constant, seemingly normative, and pervasive in the many variegated traditions of ancient Israel. This book is primally concerned with *the constant, normative, and pervasive*, because this investigation looks beyond Old Testament studies to the wider, and contemporary, theological concerns. Such a focus requires, perforce, that we leave out of consideration much of the evidence for syncretistic, heterodox, and seemingly ideosyncratic practice of worship in Israel, and focus instead on what persists and what emerges as the primal claims of worship practice in every context in Israel.

Of this preoccupation, Patrick D. Miller speaks, amid all of

5

the complex evidence, of "orthodox Yahwism" that he charac-
terizes by six accents.[16]

"Exclusive worship of the deity Yahweh was expected."[17]

"The will of the deity was conveyed by means of oracle
inquiry and prophetic audition or vision."[18]

"Sanctuaries were erected in various places ... for the
expression of devotion to the deity by means of sacrifice, festival meals and celebrations, prayer and praise."[19]

"Certain times were set for the gathering of the people to
celebrate the gifts of Yahweh and the deity's acts of deliverance and redemption."[20]

"The moral and ethical sphere was a matter of stress, with
requirements and expectations about guarding the welfare of
neighbors and providing for the weaker members of
society."[21]

"Religious leadership resided especially in the various
priests who were associated with the sanctuaries and were
dependent upon sacrifice and offering for support, but also
in prophets, who were bearers of divine oracles."[22]

Behind Miller's analysis of Israel's worship, there are of course
primal theological assumptions of which he himself has written
elsewhere. Alongside the claim of *exclusive worship*, Miller has
also observed that Israel's faith and worship are *aniconic*, that
is, without appeal to images.[23] These two marks, *exclusivity and
aniconicity*, are the primal requirements of the decalogue in
Exodus 20:3-6 and Deuteronomy 5:7-10. It should be noted that
the exclusive worship of YHWH eventuated in *monotheism*, but
the exclusionary claim of YHWH is for a long time asserted

before any formal claim of monotheism is ever voiced in Israel.[24] Thus worship in Israel is the presentation and address of all of life to this single loyalty, to the God who summons, forms, rescues, and commands Israel. The claim of YHWH upon Israel, from the outset of the encounter at Sinai, is relational long before it becomes metaphysically self-conscious or speculative. The formal metaphysical claim for the God of Israel as the only God came only later (in Second Isaiah); that, however, did not deter the passionate exclusivism of the covenantal claim from the outset.[25] If we are to understand Israel's worship rightly, then we must pay attention to the presentation of the character of God in the Old Testament texts, for whatever Israel appropriated from its environment for worship, it transposed into a vehicle for interaction with the singular God of the covenant. Thus H. H. Rowley is surely correct in his judgment: "The real meaning of worship derives in the first place from the God to whom it is directed."[26]

The exclusionary presentation of the community of YHWH to YHWH in singular loyalty in acts and words of worship must be understood in terms of the peculiar character and will of YHWH as a God *in relation.*[27] Unlike much subsequent church theology, the Old Testament has little to say about God in God's self, but much to say about God in relation. That relationship in the Old Testament is termed a "covenant," a bilateral relationship between YHWH and Israel that YHWH initiates in a generous act of commitment and self-giving.[28] Roland de Vaux witnesses to the personal character of the God of covenant,[29] and Miller judges:

> There does not seem to be any period in Israel's religious history where the specific recognition of the relation of deity and tribe or people was not expressed in such a pact, though it took different forms prior to the monarchy and during it and may have been understood or formulated differently in the North and in the South.[30]

7

It is right to say, then, that Israel's worship is to be understood as a *practice of covenant* whereby Israel variously receives and affirms the covenant, maintains and sustains the covenant, and takes steps to renew and revivify the covenant when it has been violated. It does so by various acts of gratitude and obedience, by gestures of submission and loyalty, and by words of affirmation and praise. Worship consists in words and gestures by which Israel regularly resituates its life in the ongoing narrative of YHWH who creates, judges, and rescues.[31]

This dialogic transaction that is constituted and enacted in worship requires of us an unlearning of some assumptions of conventional theology. On the one hand, the God worshiped through these acts of covenant-making, covenant-keeping, and covenant-renewing is no one-dimensional God of power as is often assumed. Rather, Israel's liturgical texts exercise great freedom and imagination in articulating YHWH in a rich variety of metaphors and figures. Among the most prominent of these are *king, warrior, judge,* and *father,* for which Israel is counterpart as subject people, rescued community, condemned or acquitted people, and children who are heirs of the promises of YHWH.[32] Less centrally, the articulation of God in the liturgic environment of Israel may utilize a number of other metaphors that open the way beyond the masculine to a God who is as nurturing as a mother.[33] In its liturgic imagination, Israel explores a rich variety of ways in which its covenantal relationship with YHWH can be presented (and practiced) in all its fullness.

On the other hand, not only do the people who worship this God in praise and in obedience gladly submit to the rule of this God who requires exclusive loyalty, but Israel is also capable of and free to seize the initiative in the relationship. Israel can engage in insistent and candid address to YHWH, thereby summoning YHWH to be faithful to YHWH's own intention and promises. In speaking of Psalm 44, Harrelson comments:

It is far from a model prayer, according to approved taste. The worshiper says in effect that he has heard that old story of God's saving deeds until he is sick of it. No doubt it is true that once God helped his people, saw to their needs, delivered Moses and the slaves from Egypt, provided a rich and good land for their descendants. But look at us now: the land lies in ruins, God's house is a shambles, we have no possibility of making a life for ourselves, and God does not care. Either he cannot any longer help; or he will not—and in both instances he falls under condemnation.

The important point here is that the worshiper says so, and says so passionately. He is as deeply involved in the act of communion with God as is the worshiper who is praising and extolling God's virtues and excellencies. His passion is aroused by the apparent injustice of God, and he pours out his soul in the act of worship. The saving history is for him a bitter irony, and he is not slow to say just that.[34]

Thus worship in Israel consists in *a dialogic interaction* in which both parties are fully present, both parties are to some extent defined by the other, and both parties are put to some extent at risk by the transaction. It is important to recognize that worship is itself the arena of such interaction in which something new in the relationship is effected through the dialogic exchange. In more rationalistic and didactic understanding of worship, it is tempting to think of worship as a reflection upon a relationship that is already settled elsewhere and fixed. Not so in ancient Israel; the act of worship is itself the transaction whereby this relationship that defines both parties is reconstituted, again and again, in decisive ways.

9

CHAPTER 2

The Gestures of Worship and Sacrifice

Israel's worship consists in regular public assembly wherein Israel performed certain freighted acts that are communal, public, and material. Through these acts Israel attested over and over again—to those within the community and to those outside the community—that it gladly participated in an exclusive, defining relationship with this God. It asserted in such acts, moreover, that this God relates to this community in a way unparalleled in any other relationship. In the acts of worship that we will consider, it is important to notice that the accent in the Old Testament, characteristically, is much more upon *the thing done* than upon *the meaning* of the thing done. The performance itself constitutes a bodily act of covenantal engagement that may over time be variously understood. The materiality of worship is an exceedingly powerful facet in this worship. It is usual to notice that the two defining acts of public worship in Israel are *the celebration of festivals* and *the offering of sacrifices*.

11

The Celebration of Festivals

Israel celebrated a fairly constant rota of festivals, though with important variations in particular textual scenarios. It is likely that these festivals in Israel did not arise *de novo;* they are, rather, appropriated from an agricultural environment that had a long-standing sequence of festivals that was geared to the varying agricultural seasons that ran from seed time to harvest, or alternatively, according to the human life cycle from birth to death. Insofar as the festival scheme arose from an agricultural context, the festivals are designed to acknowledge and celebrate the blessings of the created order through acts of worship that bespeak the reliable, generous gifts of the creator that make joyous life possible. It is likely that such a standardized scheme as is reflected in the "festal calendars" of the Old Testament had many variations. No doubt the several Old Testament texts have variously imposed an ordering on festivals that may be somewhat secondary and likely context specific. Many scholars think that the festivals that celebrate the *blessings of creation* have been "historicized" in order to focus upon the "historical deeds" of YHWH who has intervened in the public processes of history in decisive ways.[1] In the presentations that "historicize," YHWH is acknowledged as the one who *redeems* through specific acts from problematic or unbearable historical circumstance. As a result, the several festivals variously relate to YHWH as *creator* wherein the blessings of creation are acknowledged or as *redeemer* wherein historical deliverances are remembered.[2] The festival as worship is a gesture made in order to refer and relate all of life to the character and action of YHWH, the one who is known in festival as giver and transformer of life. Israel at worship thereby concedes that its own life and the life of the world are derived from and dependent upon YHWH who is the giver of every good and gracious gift.

With that Yahwistic focus, we may consider the several liturgical calendars in the Old Testament, to see that each is a program whereby every facet of life is redescribed in imaginative ways with reference to YHWH. No doubt the oldest festal calendar is in Exodus 23:14-17, augmented by verses 10-13. This list provides for the three festivals of Unleavened Bread, Harvest (elsewhere called Weeks), and a harvest festival that became Booths or Pentecost. It is clear that the latter two are agricultural, in celebration of harvest. The explanation of the significance of these feasts is very lean. The main point would seem to be, "You must show up!" in order to give visible attestation that one is publicly aligned with YHWH and with YHWH's people. This three-festival prescription is supplemented in verses 10-13 with reference to the Sabbath that is an intentional disruption of the work schedule, and then a seven-year ingathering especially designed for the care of the poor.[3] On this latter point, the worship of Israel, in this very early outline, concerns alertness to profound human need. It is not too much to observe that this lean mention of "the poor" (*'ebyon*) in Israel's earliest catalogue, with the addition of concern for the "homeborn slave" and "resident alien" in the Sabbath provision (v. 12), stands at the beginning of a trajectory indicating that worship is never an end in itself. It characteristically issues a "missional" summons to Israel to be actively engaged in compassion for the needy in society. This inchoate missional accent, it seems clear, comes to fruition in the polemical characterization of worship for its own sake (Isa 58:1-5) and an urgent turn toward the "homeless poor" (*'ani merur*) in Isaiah 58:6-7.[4]

A second early liturgical calendar in Exodus 34:18-26 again revolves around the three festivals of Unleavened Bread, Weeks, and Ingathering with the injunction, "Three times in the year all your males shall appear before the LORD God, the God of Israel" (v. 23).

One is struck again by the terseness of the requirement. While the detail of practice is somewhat fuller here and a reference to Sabbath in verse 21 intrudes upon the three festivals,

13

the text offers no interpretation of the festivals. The men must show up! The other accent that will become commonplace is: "No one shall appear before me empty-handed [*riq*]" (v. 20). It is clear that the agricultural festivals included bringing gifts of produce back to YHWH in the sanctuary in an acknowledgment that the creator God has given blessing, and that Israel is a generous, grateful people that does not retain all such blessings for itself.

The third calendar in Deuteronomy 16:1-17 shows development and variation, this time reflective of the quite distinctive theological passion of the Deuteronomic tradition. Now the practice of Unleavened Bread is linked to Passover, a festival that remembers, narrates, and contemporizes the deliverance from Egypt (16:1-8; see Exod 12–13). This is the most dramatic "historicizing" of the celebrations of the blessings of creation, for now the festival pertains to an historical deliverance and the continuing reality of being YHWH's emancipated people. The text assumes a "Passover sacrifice." The Festival of Weeks anticipated a "freewill offering" (16:10) so that the entire community may rejoice, including,

> You and your sons and your daughters, your male and female slaves, the Levites resident in your towns, as well as the strangers, the orphans, and the widows who are among you. (v. 11)

This provision resituated the community in an Exodus reality (v. 12). In the third festival, the Festival of Booths, the celebration relates to harvest, and again enumerates the socially marginalized who are the special object of care (vv. 11-12). Now (a) everyone must show up (16:16), (b) not empty-handed, and (c) for the sake of the needy. The festival is public acknowledgment that the life of the entire community is a gift of the God who blesses. Thus the practitioners of festival mediate between the God who blesses and the community in its need. That

14

mediation is a call to disciplined generosity for the sake of "the others."

Just as Deuteronomy 16:1-17 reflects the interests and passions of the Deuteronomic tradition with its focus on the needy in the community, so the fourth calendar, that of Leviticus 23:4-44, reflects the quite different interests and passions of the Priestly tradition. In Leviticus 23, provisions for three festivals are more clearly ordered and elaborated in great detail. The summary statement of Leviticus 23:37-38 is a fuller form of what we have already seen in earlier texts, but with a more comprehensive notion of offerings:

> These are the appointed festivals of the LORD, which you shall celebrate as times of holy convocation, for presenting to the LORD offerings by fire—burnt offerings and grain offerings, sacrifices and drink offerings, each on its proper day—apart from the sabbaths of the LORD, and apart from your gifts, and apart from all your votive offerings, and apart from all your freewill offerings, which you give to the LORD. (Lev 23:37-38)

The detail of this calendar again concerns Unleavened Bread (vv. 5-14), Weeks (vv. 15-22), and Booths (vv. 33-43); interspersed among these three, however, is reference to the "Day of Atonement" presented in terms of Sabbath rest (see vv. 23-32) plus a promise for the poor that is not immediately linked to the festival but to the harvest that evokes the festival. Thus even in the Priestly tradition with its preoccupation with cultic matters, the concern for neighbor is voiced. These assemblies are termed "Holy Convocations" (*miqra'e qodesh*); the term makes clear that Israel at worship is a holy people which in context means singularly devoted to YHWH, ordered in clean, pure ways congruent with YHWH's own holiness. Thus festivals are occasions of disciplined holiness.[5]

Finally, in Numbers 28–29, a fuller catalogue of festivals is offered. In a much more complex account that is preoccupied with technique, the same three festivals are primary: Passover with Unleavened Bread (28:16-25), Weeks (28:26-31), and Booths (29:12-38). Three accents in addition may be noted in this account: (a) the entire process of festival participates in holiness, (b) there is great stress upon "no work," and (c) there is great precision about the particular regimen of sacrifices. The aim of the whole is to generate a community of holiness that is completely devoted in concrete ways to YHWH. Two signs of that holiness are enjoined. First, "no work" means to disengage from the world of production and control, in order to be in a receptive mode for the blessings of the creator. Second, the practice of sacrifice, outlined in detail and with punctiliousness, is perhaps the counterpoint to "no work"; sacrifice entails *offering back to* YHWH a part of the blessing YHWH has given, thus making clear in public ways that life is a gift; the character of holiness is to dramatize the gift of YHWH by being in turn generous toward YHWH.

These several inventories provide very different nuances to gestures of festival, depending upon the interpretive horizon of a particular tradition. This is most evident in the differing accents of the Deuteronomic and the Priestly traditions (Deut 16:1-17; Lev 23:4-44; Num 28–29).[6] Nonetheless, all of these calendars insist upon a structure of three festivals (with supplements of various kinds), all of them require showing up in public, and most include an offering of some substance in response to the gifts of YHWH. In sum, all of them intend that this distinctive community of YHWH must live out in visible, palpable, material ways—in thick, freighted symbolization—the peculiar, defining mark of covenant. The texts voice some urgency about showing up, aware that without regular, public, visible, thick symbolization, the community of Israel would soon disappear into the woodwork of a religious environment that, from the perspective of these imperatives, has about it nothing of gratitude, holiness, or missional attentiveness to the needy. The festivals, by their very performance, serve to generate and sustain a community with a quite distinct ethos, a community that did not exist and could not be sustained without such thick, intentional symbolization. It is no wonder that not showing up for the festival is taken as tantamount to ceasing to be Israel!

These three festivals, in quite varied articulation, constitute the "church year" in ancient Israel. In these acts, Israel subsumes all of its life—the blessings of creation and the rescues of history—and refers all of its life back to YHWH, for the festivals are characteristically "for YHWH" *(leyhwh)*. In the midst of that consistent practice, it is clear that the liturgical calendar is open, in different seasons and in different contexts, to supplementation, in order that the community—or some subcommunity within Israel—can enact its particular experience of covenant with YHWH. In addition to Sabbath that permeates these instructions, we may notice four other festivals that do not permeate the tradition but that are undoubtedly important in particular contexts.

(1) *The Day of Atonement (Yom Kippur)* in Leviticus 16:30 is unknown in the earlier calendars but mentioned, as we have seen, in Leviticus 23:26-32. It is clear that this festival emerged—and became central in subsequent Judaism—because it provided reconciliation to YHWH for a community that found itself deeply alienated from YHWH and without resources of its own for redress of that alienation. The festival is a provision of grace whereby YHWH provided a mechanism for reconciliation. The detail of Leviticus 16 is preoccupied with techniques for implementation; the point should not be lost, however, that from YHWH's side a way is provided to overcome Israel's breach of holiness. While the techniques are important in the texts (and no doubt to the priests who enacted them), the important point is the massive theological affirmation through the festival. It is to be noted, moreover, that in the book of Hebrews, in chapters 7–10, the entire framing of the work of Christ is according to the festival procedure, culminating in Hebrews 9:23-28 wherein Christ "bears the sins of many." This

17

interpretation of the work of Christ, to be sure, voices a polemical supersessionism against the claims of Judaism. At the same time, however, the claim made for Christ depends completely upon the rhetoric and vision of the tradition of Leviticus. Judaism and Christianity hold in common that the God worshiped among us both wills reconciliation and restoration of covenant and provides a costly, generous means of such reconciliation and restoration.

(2) We have seen that reference to Sabbath is pervasive in these calendars. It is only in Leviticus 25, however, that the celebration of *Jubilee* is prescribed, a schedule of "seven times seven" years wherein land shall be returned to its rightful heir. This is not only an odd provision. It is likely the most radical "festival" in the Old Testament, one providing that Israel's devotion to YHWH takes form and shape in the public affairs of political economy.[7] While the Jubilee is "for you" (Lev 25:10), it is clear that the practice is rooted in the Sabbath provision that asserts that life does not consist in production and acquisition, but in the reception of gifts from YHWH mediated through the community. The claim of the Jubilee year is that the heirs of land cannot be denied what is theirs. The festival is a promise and guarantee of entitlement that is an antidote to an acquisitive political economy that is not deeply rooted in covenantal symbolization. To the extent that Jubilee may be regarded as a festival of worship, it indicates the way in which thick gestures made in response to YHWH inevitably spill over into the life of the world in transformative ways.

(3) The festival of *Purim* is a late emergent in the Old Testament and is rooted textually only in Esther 9:18-32. The festival emerged, according to the narrative, to celebrate and commemorate "the days in which the Jews gained relief from their enemies" (Esth 9:22).

Thus it is a celebration of the distinctiveness of the Jewish community that is characteristically under threat, but rescued— in this case—by human wit rooted in loyalty to YHWH. It is worth noting that the celebration includes "presents to the poor" (Esth

9:22). The festival, since that time and now with contemporary urgency, has become important in the maintenance and sustenance of Jewish identity in a world heavy with risk.

(4) The festival of *Hanukkah*, legitimated outside the canon in 1 Maccabees 4:36-59, arose in connection with the rededication of the Jerusalem Temple after the profanation of it by the Syrians. I cite this festival only to note that festivals in particular times and places, in response to particular communal crises, continue to emerge in the practice of Judaism. Clearly this community has understood from the outset that all of life—characterized by the blessings of creation and the rescues of history—needed to be redescribed in faith by signs that derive from and in turn sign life back to YHWH in gratitude and obedience.

These four belated festivals that stretch all the way from an acute sense of *holiness recovered* (Yom Kippur) to *neighborhood reconstituted* (Jubilee) evidence the free range of Israel's liturgical imagination in reenacting all of life and thereby reconstituting all of life in a world governed by YHWH. The three basic festivals provide spine and structure for the larger festal calendar with which Israel continued to experiment. Thus we are given a structure and a sequence that is open to innovation.

This threefold structure, moreover, with only a slight imaginative transposition, can be readily taken up in the church as the three great festivals of Christmas, Easter, and Pentecost. In Christian practice these festivals are acutely christological; they are, however, at the same time also rooted in the deepest routines of creation. By *showing up at festivals*, the worshiping community gladly resituates, redescribes, and reconstitutes its life as life in a world over which YHWH powerfully and graciously presides.

The Offering of Sacrifices

Old Testament worship is characteristically marked by the offering of sacrifices—the presentation of something of material value by the community to YHWH. The presentation of some-thing of material value is understood as a response of the com-munity to the reality of YHWH, to the gracious sustenance assured by YHWH, and to the powerful interventions YHWH has taken in forming and summoning the life of Israel. It is likely, as has long been held in Old Testament study, that the ordered practice of sacrifice developed over time from ad hoc practices to a quite rigorously prescribed inventory of various sacrifices that were implemented in different modes and designed for a variety of functions and purposes.

All through that development, nonetheless, the same inten-tion is operative, namely, to interact with and respond to YHWH in ways that maintain, enhance, or reconstitute a covenantal relationship with YHWH. We have seen that in the Priestly man-dates of Leviticus 23 (especially vv. 37-38) and in Numbers 29:12-38 concerning the Festival of Booths, the festival is an occasion for offerings and sacrifices. The texts show the way in which our "first gesture" of festival and now our "second ges-ture" of sacrifice are connected. The festival is appropriately the venue and occasion for sacrifice. A full inventory of sacrifices is offered in Leviticus 1–7 in which nuance and detail of the sev-eral sacrifices are given with enormous care in order to make distinctions and to preclude distortion.

It is commonly agreed that the sacrifices offered by Israel to YHWH serve three important intentions in the service of the covenant between the two parties.

(1) Sacrifice is the presentation of *gift*, an act of recognition, generosity, and gratitude toward YHWH who is the initial giver of all that Israel has. The offer of a gift not only situates Israel before YHWH in an act of committed generosity, but also charac-terizes YHWH as the primal and quintessential giver (1 Chr 29:14; 1 Cor 4:7). The presentation of a material gift of value (characteristically a sacrifice "without blemish") costs the wor-shiper in an act that binds the worshiper to YHWH. In a careful-ly worded observation, De Vaux suggests that such an act is not

disinterested, for in making the offering, the worshiper "gains something, for the acceptance of the gift involves God in an obligation."[8] Thus the act of gift giving is an act that binds, characteristically a mix of gladness and of calculation (on which see, for example, Gen 28:20-22).

(2) The offering of animal and vegetable sacrifices creates an occasion for a meal, and a meal is the quintessential social occasion of being with another in joy and well-being. Thus the sacrifice is an act of *communion* wherein Israel can "enjoy" the company of YHWH (see Exod 24:11). The offer of something of value may be understood as an offering that is wholly consumed by the deity as "whole burnt offering." Or conversely, it can be food that is, in the end, given to the poor of the community, thus creating a communion for the entire community. Such a meal is not only a sign of solidarity, but an event in that ongoing solidarity.

(3) There are, in Israel's liturgic practice, need for acts of *expiation* whereby Israel's disobedience or violation of holiness has created a palpable impediment to communion with YHWH. The impediment may be understood relationally as a violation of covenant that has broken the relationship that now needs to be repaired and is repaired by a gesture of self-giving generosity; or the impediment may otherwise be understood in more material terms as a foreign element that renders the community polluted so that the material presence of YHWH becomes impossible in such an environment. In such an understanding that is characteristic of the Priestly tradition, what is unholy or unclean must be purged for the sake of recovered purity. In context, the "sin offering" and "guilt offering" may be understood as acts of purgation or purification whereby a restored relationship is possible and the presence of YHWH, the holy God, can again be entertained.

Two things strike one about this characterization of these offerings. First, characteristically *nothing is said* that explains the act of sacrifice. As with the festivals, it is the action of sacrifice, the public gesture itself, to which attention is paid. Such a reticence about commentary on the act indicates that it is the material thing done that is efficacious; this lack of commentary also means that the acts and gestures of sacrifice—not unlike the Eucharist in Christian practice—are left open to a variety of interpretations; the communal act leaves the theological meaning and intent of the act quite open. Second, the deed of sacrifice is *powerfully efficacious,* an act performed whereby the status of the relation between the two covenant partners is decisively impacted. In the very process of the act, the relationship becomes something that it was not prior to the act.

The *absence of interpretive comment* on the gestures of sacrifice and *the efficaciousness of the act in itself* of course left open the possibility that sacrifices could come to be regarded as mechanical acts that could automatically "fix" the covenantal relationship. There is no doubt that that could happen in Israel, and we are free to hunch that it did in fact happen on occasion. The prophetic polemics against such liturgic acts characteristically condemn sacrifices that have become pro forma performances without serious covenantal engagement (see 1 Sam 15:22-23; Isa 1:11-15; Jer 7:4; Hos 6:6; Amos 4:4-5; Mic 6:6-8). It is a common judgment of scholars that such polemics are not aimed at liturgical *use,* but at liturgical *abuse* wherein the performed act is separated from the reality of covenantal relationship. And wherever that happened, the worship of Israel simply devolved into the generic religious performance of its cultural environment.

We may in particular notice the reference to sacrifice in the twinned Psalms 50 and 51. Psalm 50, likely a liturgical outline for a service of covenantal renewal, is at pains to insist that YHWH has no need of Israel's sacrifices, for YHWH as creator already governs a world full of creaturely goods and Israel can supply nothing for the creator God (Ps 50:8-13). In light of that claim, it is worth noticing that in verses 14-15, 23 the community of Israel is nonetheless enjoined to bring "a sacrifice of thanksgiving" in order to demonstrate dependence upon YHWH and gratitude to YHWH. Clearly there are sacrifices that are appropriate to covenantal worship and sacrifices that are objectionable. In Psalm 51, the speaker confesses sin and recognizes that YHWH wants a repentant heart and not a material offering:

> O Lord, open my lips,
> > and my mouth will declare your praise.
> For you have no delight in sacrifice;
> > if I were to give a burnt offering, you would not be pleased.
> The sacrifice acceptable to God is a broken spirit;
> > a broken and contrite heart,
> > O God, you will not despise. (vv. 16-17)

But then, in a conclusion that is perhaps an addendum to the psalm, the psalm reverses field, acknowledging that God will delight in sacrifice:[9]

> Do good to Zion in your good pleasure;
> > rebuild the walls of Jerusalem,
> then you will delight in right sacrifices,
> > in burnt offerings and whole burnt offerings;
> > then bulls will be offered on your altar. (v. 18-19)

The juxtaposition of verses 18-19 alongside verses 16-17 demonstrates the tricky judgment Israel made about sacrifices; sacrifices are carriers of right faith, but dangerously open to misuse. Israel clearly had two decisive perceptions about sacrifice. First, worship is about a *relationship* and everything must serve that relationship; second, that relationship must be given *concrete, material articulation*. A tradition of pietism, as the one in which the author is located, will of course appreciate the first accent on the relationship at the expense of the second. This practice of faith and worship, however, is aware that the materiality of life matters decisively in worship; in the end this worship cannot do without costly material gestures. These gestures bind the community to the creator God who forgives and begins again with Israel.

CHAPTER 3

The Utterance of YHWH in Worship

The gestures of worship we have reviewed are likely borrowed from the cultural environment in which Israel lived. The specific acts of festival and sacrifice, for the most part, had no distinguishing Israelite or Yahwistic features in and of themselves, being simply reflective of generic usage. Those gestures, however, never occur by themselves; they are always accompanied by utterances that interpret the gestures and that identify in those gestures the specificity and particularity that cause the gestures to be effective vehicles for Israel's faith. Thus it is always *utterance with gesture*, always *word with sacrament* wherein the generic is made suitably specific to Israel's covenantal faith.[1]

The worship of Israel may be understood as a covenantal conversation, perhaps best taken as a dialogue enacted in antiphonic ways. Both parties to the covenant, YHWH through priestly mediators and Israel, have their say in utterances designed to further the relationship that lives in and through such liturgic reiteration. In this chapter and the next, we will consider in turn the *utterances of YHWH* and *of Israel* that together constitute the word that identifies sacramental action as Yahwistic and covenantal.

From the outset, YHWH is a God who discloses God's self in utterance. Clearly such utterances, in the regular cadences of worship, are stylized and mediated through authorized human speech.[2] The utterances of YHWH are nonetheless self-disclosing of YHWH's will and purpose. We may identify two sorts of utterances on the lips of YHWH that are to be regularly heard, received, and embraced by Israel. The God who speaks in worship is the God who *commands, guides,* and *assures.*

First, YHWH, the sovereign Lord of the covenant, declares the divine will through the *utterance of commandments,* a series of imperatives presented as the conditions of the covenant, or alternatively, as appropriate responses to the free gift of covenant that Israel is to undertake. Either way, the God whom Israel meets in worship, as the tradition is now constructed, is the God of Sinai. The meeting at Sinai is the model for subsequent worship assemblies in Israel wherein Israel engages with YHWH in covenantal interaction. At Sinai, and so with subsequent worship assemblies, YHWH is present through a great theophanic intrusion (Exod 19:16-25; see Ps 50:1-3). When YHWH speaks at the mountain, it is in order to utter the divine will for Israel in ten commandments (Exod 20:1-17; Deut 5:6-21). These commands, YHWH's first utterance to Israel in worship, provide the most elemental, non-negotiable, absolute requirements for Israel's life as YHWH's people.[3] The import of the Decalogue is to bring every sphere of life under the rule of YHWH.

According to the tradition of Deuteronomy that comes to dominate the theme of Torah in the Old Testament, it is most probable that Israel assembled regularly—in relation to the festivals we have considered—in order to hear the commands of YHWH reiterated and to make fresh assent to them (see Deut 31:9-13). Psalm 81, moreover, is commonly taken to be a residue of what must have been a regular, periodic assembly for covenant-making and renewal (see also Pss 50, 95).[4] Psalm 81:4-10 appears to replicate the utterance of YHWH at Sinai. In verses

6-7, YHWH recalls for Israel past deliverances enacted by YHWH. This utterance is dominated by YHWH as the first-person subject of the decisive verbs in a way that is parallel to Exodus 20:2. Then follow the covenantal imperative dominated by the word "hear" (*shema'*). Israel's proper stance in worship is to listen with a proclivity to obey. The second half of verse 8 rebukes Israel for "not listening," and so implies that the covenant has been violated. But verse 9 reiterates the dominant command of Sinai "no other gods" and so invites Israel back into covenant, a covenant of obedience. Verse 10 then identifies the One who speaks as the God of the Exodus who will bless Israel. It is clear that verses 9-10 reiterate Exodus 20:2-3, only with the two rhetorical elements ("I am YHWH ... no other gods") now inverted. The remainder of the psalm invites Israel to *listen* (v. 13), that is, to respond to the commands and thereby to receive yet again YHWH's good blessings (vv. 14-16). Everything in this encounter turns on the command of YHWH that seeks the banishment of other gods (v. 9) and Israel's response to the divine utterance.

The commands of YHWH are frequently and regularly reasserted to remind Israel in worship of its peculiar destiny as a people under YHWH's command. It is clear from the shape of the Torah tradition, however, that Israel in worship did not simply hear again "the big ten." The extensive Torah material in the Pentateuch indicates that the Decalogue was not only reiterated but interpreted, extended, and extrapolated over time.[5] It is fair to conclude that a primary venue for such interpretive extrapolation was worship wherein the basic commands of YHWH are made contemporary. The reference to the Levites as the ones who "teach Jacob your ordinances and Israel your laws" suggests that the priestly office includes the work of Torah instruction, perhaps in response to the casting of lots (*Thummim* and *Urim*) (Deut 33:8-10).[6] The Priestly teachers, especially in the book of Leviticus, extrapolated the significance of holiness for every aspect of Israel's life.[7] We are able to see more clearly in the tradition of Deuteronomy that the Torah is made contemporary through interpretation that extends the commands in considerable detail:[8] "Not with our ancestors did the LORD make this covenant, but with us, who are all of us here alive today" (Deut 5:3). Thus at the outset of this tradition, Moses "expounds this Torah" (Deut 1:5). At the latter end of the same tradition, Ezra and the Levites interpret this same Torah. They,

> Jeshua, Bani, Sherebiah, Jamin, Akkub, Shabbethai, Hodiah, Maaseiah, Kelita, Azariah, Jozabad, Hanan, Pelaiah, the Levites, helped the people to understand the law, while the people remained in their places. So they read from the book, from the law of God, with interpretation. They gave the sense, so that the people understood the reading. (Neh 8:7-8)

On this basis, we may imagine that ongoing worship in Israel was greatly preoccupied with elucidating the commands of Sinai. Indeed, Gerhard von Rad has characterized the material of the commandments in Deuteronomy as "preached law," that is, as the requirement of YHWH given with some homiletical twist.[9] It is too much to say that this material constitutes "sermons," but such nomenclature is not far off the mark if "sermon" is understood as elucidation of treasured texts for the sake of contemporaneity. The material in Deuteronomy 6–8 and Jeremiah 7, 18:1-11, and 24:1-10, all of which bear the marks of the Deuteronomic tradition, are something like sermon material. These texts characteristically voice the urgent "either/or" that marks the covenantal instruction of Sinai and of Deuteronomy. The purpose of such sermonic address is that the assembled people should depart the meeting, freshly situated in the world of YHWH's commands, and thus in the matrix of YHWH's will for the world.

Second, the God who speaks in the worship of Israel articulates oracles that offer both *guidance and assurance*. These oracles are given in stylized rhetorical patterns. In each case they are pertinent to the assembly of the day. We may distinguish two sorts of oracles, though in fact both function to place YHWH front and center as sovereign in the ongoing life of Israel.

YHWH issues *oracles of guidance* when Israel must make decisions about its life and its future. The priestly office charged with such oracles is accepted as having access to the divine will and purpose in a way that was, in context, taken to be trustworthy.[10] On the one hand, there is evidence that such priestly oracles aided in sorting out the requirements and boundaries of holiness that were taken to be life-or-death matters:

> Thus says the LORD of hosts: Ask the priests for a ruling: If one carries consecrated meat in the fold of one's garment, and with the fold touches bread, or stew, or wine, or oil, or any kind of food, does it become holy? The priests answered, "No." Then Haggai said, "If one who is unclean by contact with a dead body touches any of these, does it become unclean?" The priests answered, "Yes, it becomes unclean." (Hag 2:11-13)

*　*　*

> Now the people of Bethel had sent Sharezer and Regemmelech and their men, to entreat the favor of the LORD, and to ask the priests of the house of the LORD of hosts and the prophets, "Should I mourn and practice abstinence in the fifth month, as I have done for so many years?" Then the word of the LORD of hosts came to me: Say to all the people of the land and the priests: When you fasted and lamented in the fifth month and in the seventh, for these seventy years, was it for me that you fasted? And when you eat and when you drink, do you not eat and drink only for yourselves? Were not these the words that the LORD proclaimed by the former prophets, when Jerusalem was inhabited and in prosperity, along with the towns around it, and when the Negeb and the Shephelah were inhabited? (Zech 7:2-7)

29

The priests' function in this context is not unlike medical doctors in contemporary life. They gave guidance on choices that would make for health, but they did not offer detailed, technical explanations for their judgments.

On the other hand, in some earlier contexts, the priests issued oracles of guidance to kings concerning royal policy. The narrative of 1 Kings 22 concerning Micaiah ben Imlah is an extended account of an oracle of guidance. In that narrative the other prophets gave the royal coalition an easy, expected response to the royal inquiry:

> All the prophets were prophesying the same and saying, "Go up to Ramothgilead and triumph; the Lord will give it into the hand of the king." (1 Kgs 22:12)

In their suspicion, however, the kings also inquired of Micaiah, who gave them a more difficult response, indicating that divine oracle could be given with freedom that subverted the expectation of the inquiry (1 Kgs 22:13-28). In less complex fashion, a direct answer to such inquiry may be terse and to the point:

> After this David inquired of the Lord, "Shall I go up into any of the cities of Judah?" The Lord said to him, "Go up." David said, "To which shall I go up?" He said, "To Hebron." (2 Sam 2:1)

It is this easy access and positive expectation that prompts King Zedekiah, in his desperation, to make inquiry of Jeremiah:

> Please inquire of the Lord on our behalf, for King Nebuchadrezzar of Babylon is making war against us; perhaps the Lord will perform a wonderful deed for us, as he has often done, and will make him withdraw from us. (Jer 21:2)

Against royal expectation, Jeremiah's oracle of guidance is a hard one:

Then Jeremiah said to them: Thus you shall say to Zedekiah: Thus says the LORD, the God of Israel: I am going to turn back the weapons of war that are in your hands and with which you are fighting against the king of Babylon and against the Chaldeans who are besieging you outside the walls; and I will bring them together into the center of this city. I myself will fight against you with outstretched hand and mighty arm, in anger, in fury, and in great wrath. And I will strike down the inhabitants of this city, both human beings and animals; they shall die of a great pestilence. Afterward, says the LORD, I will give King Zedekiah of Judah, and his servants, and the people in this city—those who survive the pestilence, sword, and famine—into the hands of King Nebuchadrezzar of Babylon, into the hands of their enemies, into the hands of those who seek their lives. He shall strike them down with the edge of the sword; he shall not pity them, or spare them, or have compassion. (Jer 21:3-7)

* * *

Then King Zedekiah sent for him, and received him. The king questioned him secretly in his house, and said, "Is there any word from the LORD?" Jeremiah said, "There is!" Then he said, "You shall be handed over to the king of Babylon." (Jer 37:17)

It is clear that oracular capacity was shared by priests and prophets in a way that cannot be easily sorted out. It is, moreover, not clear that all of these oracles are situated in a worship assembly.[11] We may, however, accept the worship assembly as the venue in which the utterance of YHWH could most probably be available, even if this same practice was also undertaken outside such assemblies.

YHWH issues *oracles of assurance*. By far the greater number of divine oracles are designed to offer assurance of YHWH's transformative presence in circumstances of threat and risk, thereby offering hope and possibility in contexts that appear to be

31

hopeless and impossible.[12] This element of worship has most in common with contemporary "assurance of pardon," even though Israel was not, as in such a contemporary rubric, preoccupied with issues of guilt and forgiveness. These oracles, in the mouth of some trusted officer of the worshiping community, are offered in response to an utterance of petition, confession, or protest. In these texts YHWH is the one who answers with authority in order to transpose and transform the context of the petitioner by utterance. It is not evident that such oracles are characteristically in cultic assemblies, but we may consider the sanctuary as a model venue for practice that may also have occurred in a variety of other contexts.

As we shall see below, Israel boldly articulated its needs and its helplessness to YHWH who was taken to be a help "when other helpers fail and comforts flee." Such petitions are voiced in narrative contexts such as Genesis 15:1-6 and 32:9-12. In the case of Hannah, her petition to YHWH is addressed in a sanctuary:

> She was deeply distressed and prayed to the LORD, and wept bitterly. She made this vow: "O LORD of hosts, if only you will look on the misery of your servant, and remember me, and not forget your servant, but will give to your servant a male child, then I will set him before you as a nazarite until the day of his death. He shall drink neither wine nor intoxicants, and no razor shall touch his head." (1 Sam 1:10-11)

Hannah's petition for a son that she herself cannot produce is a desperate, concrete, trustful request grounded in the conviction that YHWH hears and that YHWH is indeed able to enact such a transformative wonder. Her prayer is characteristic of the bold petition of Israel. Our concern here, however, is with the divine oracle of response that is on the lips of the priest, Eli: "Then Eli answered, 'Go in peace; the God of Israel grant the petition you have made to him'" (1 Sam 1:17). Eli offers a divine assurance that acknowledges Hannah's petition and that promises to deliver on her request. As the narrative subsequently unfolds, it is clear that Eli's oracle is effective and alters her future. YHWH is responsive and reliable, attentive to the petition and capable of delivery.

As Patrick Miller has shown, the Psalms are permeated with such petitions to which a divine oracle is an effective response.[13] Representative is the oracle reported in Psalm 35:3 in which the speaker offers a cue for what YHWH is to say in response:

> Contend, O LORD, with those who contend with me;
> > fight against those who fight against me!
> Take hold of shield and buckler,
> > and rise up to help me!
> Draw the spear and javelin against my pursuers;
> say to my soul, "I am your salvation." (Ps 35:1-3)

Israel gladly reports that YHWH has heard and answered:

> Depart from me, all you workers of evil,
> > for the LORD has heard the sound of my weeping.
> The LORD has heard my supplication;
> > the LORD accepts my prayer. (Ps 6:8-9)
> > > *   *   *

> In my distress I called upon the LORD;
> > to my God I cried for help.
> From his temple he heard my voice,
> > and my cry to him reached his ears. (Ps 18:6)[14]
> > > *   *   *

> I sought the LORD, and he answered me,
> > and delivered me from all my fears.
> Look to him, and be radiant;
> > so your faces shall never be ashamed.
> This poor soul cried, and was heard by the LORD,
> > and was saved from every trouble. (Ps 34:4-6)
> > > *   *   *

33

I waited patiently for the LORD;
>   he inclined to me and heard my cry.
He drew me up from the desolate pit,
>   out of the miry bog,
and set my feet upon a rock,
>   making my steps secure.
He put a new song in my mouth,
>   a song of praise to our God.
Many will see and fear,
>   and put their trust in the LORD. (Ps 40:1-3)

* * *

Let me hear what God the LORD will speak,
>   for he will speak peace to his people,
>   to his faithful, to those who
>   turn to him in their hearts. (Ps 85:8)

These oracles of assurance that set new life in motion occur everywhere in Israel's narrative life. But it is clear that the sixth century exile is the paradigmatic "depth" of Israel's life, and therefore the context that evokes the greatest cluster of divine oracles of assurance.[15] The quintessential example of *petition heard and answered* is in Lamentations 3:55-57:

I called on your name, O LORD,
>   from the depths of the pit;
you heard my pleas, "Do not close your ear
>   to my cry for help, but give me relief!"
You came near when I called on you;
>   you said, "Do not fear!"

The climactic divine utterance "Do not fear" is situation-transforming. This assurance on the lips of YHWH is an attestation that Israel is not alone in its displacement, not abandoned, and therefore not hopeless. The declaration of divine attentiveness to Israel in "the depth of the pit" is sufficient ground for Israel to take hopeful action and to resituate itself

34

in the buoyancy of that covenantal relationship that persists even in displacement.

The same exilic venue for divine assurance is evident in the tradition of Jeremiah:

But as for you, have no fear, my servant Jacob, says the LORD,
    and do not be dismayed, O Israel;
for I am going to save you from far away,
    and your offspring from the land of their captivity.
Jacob shall return and have quiet and ease,
    and no one shall make him afraid.
For I am with you, says the LORD, to save you;

I will make an end of all the nations
    among which I scattered you,
    but of you I will not make an end. (Jer 30:10-11a)

*   *   *

But as for you, have no fear, my servant Jacob,
    and do not be dismayed, O Israel;
for I am going to save you from far away,
    and your offspring from the land of their captivity.
Jacob shall return and have quiet and ease,
    and no one shall make him afraid.
As for you, have no fear, my servant Jacob,
        says the LORD,
    for I am with you.
I will make an end of all the nations
    among which I have banished you,
    but I will not make an end of you! (Jer 46:27-28a)

And even more spectacularly the exilic poetry of Second Isaiah offered a rich collection of such oracles:

But you, Israel, my servant,
    Jacob, whom I have chosen,
    the offspring of Abraham, my friend;

35

you whom I took from the ends of the earth,
    and called from its farthest corners,
saying to you, "You are my servant,
    I have chosen you and not cast you off";
do not fear, for I am with you,
    do not be afraid, for I am your God;
I will strengthen you, I will help you,
    I will uphold you with my victorious right hand.
Yes, all who are incensed against you
    shall be ashamed and disgraced;
those who strive against you
    shall be as nothing and shall perish.
You shall seek those who contend with you,
    but you shall not find them;
those who war against you shall be as nothing at all.
For I, the LORD your God,
    hold your right hand;
it is I who say to you, "Do not fear,
    I will help you." (Isa 41:8-13)

*   *   *

But now thus says the LORD,
    he who created you, O Jacob,
    he who formed you, O Israel:
Do not fear, for I have redeemed you;
    I have called you by name, you are mine....
Do not fear, for I am with you;
    I will bring your offspring from the east,
    and from the west I will gather you. (Isa 43:1, 5; see also
    44:8)

The priestly utterance of oracle permitted the petitioner (or the petitioning community) to depart the assembly transformed. The life of the petitioner had been resituated in the sphere of Israel's powerful, attentive, faithful God. The oracles characteristically begin with an assurance of divine presence. They regularly move, however, to declare concrete transformative actions to be undertaken by Yhwh that are to follow from the assurance of presence.

It is clear that by *utterance of command* and by *utterance of assurance* Yhwh was known to be palpably present in and engaged on behalf of the community, summoning and willing well-being for Israel of the sort Eli had offered Hannah (1 Sam 1:17). This redescription of life under the rule of Yhwh enacted in the cult of course required (a) *showing up* regularly in the assembly in order to stay within the narrative of Yhwh, and (b) having *trustworthy priests* whose word could be taken as true, reliable, and future generating. Israel was beset by "the powers of the night"—political, social, mythological—before which it was helpless. It departed such worship confident of a faithful presence that was stronger than all those powers that could not, given the divine utterance, prevail (see Jer 1:17-19; 15:20; 20:11-13).[16]

CHAPTER 4

The Utterance of Israel
in Worship

Israel at worship was not docile, passive, or silent. It was deeply engaged in a life-or-death verbal interaction with YHWH in which its future was profoundly at stake. For that reason, Israel vigorously held up its end of the covenantal conversation, sometimes in response to the utterances and actions of YHWH, sometimes boldly taking the initiative with YHWH.

(1) Israel's primal utterance in worship is *an act of remembering* that is implicitly an act of hope. In such utterance Israel anticipates that the future will feature more of the decisive transformative goodness of YHWH that Israel had known in the past. Thus the centerpiece of such communal utterance, as Gerhard von Rad has shown, is a regularized (soon to be canonical) normative narrative of YHWH's past goodnesses to Israel.[1]

As we have seen, the festival calendars for the most part provide no words for Israel to speak in its gestures of celebration. At the most there are allusions to the Exodus (Exod 23:15; Lev 23:42; Deut 16:3, 6, 12) and to the gift of the land (Exod 34:24). These allusions help draw the festivals to Israel's particularity, but only with hints. There are other texts, however, in which *utterance* is crucial to *gesture*. In Deuteronomy 26:5-9, as von Rad has famously underscored, the offering of firstfruits is accompanied by a narrative that articulates Israel's primal memory of Egypt and the gift of the land.[2] In Exodus 12–13, moreover, the Passover is given rich narrative substance in the form of instruction to the children concerning the concrete significance of the festival:

> And when your children ask you, "What do you mean by this observance?" you shall say, "It is the Passover sacrifice to the LORD, for he passed over the houses of the Israelites in Egypt, when he struck down the Egyptians but spared our houses." And the people bowed down and worshiped. (Exod 12:26-27)

*   *   *

> You shall tell your child on that day, "It is because of what the LORD did for me when I came out of Egypt." (Exod 13:8)

*   *   *

> When in the future your child asks you, "What does this mean?" you shall answer, "By strength of hand the LORD brought us out of Egypt, from the house of slavery. When Pharaoh stubbornly refused to let us go, the LORD killed all the firstborn in the land of Egypt, from human firstborn to the firstborn of animals. Therefore I sacrifice to the LORD every male that first opens the womb, but every firstborn of my sons I redeem." (Exod 13:14-15)

In all these texts Israel boldly gives an account of its founding memory in which the life of Israel exists wholly as a result of YHWH's generous, transformative action. For good reason von Rad termed this recital a "credo," for the utterance is a stylized confessional act of commitment whereby Israel takes sides theologically, risks its identity and its future on YHWH's capacity, and refuses alternative accounts of reality that were surely available in a Canaanite environment.[3] It is credible to imagine that the festivals, though prescribed without utterance, were the primal venues in which Israel recounted its past to the children and in which Israel acknowledged YHWH to be the "fertility God" who has given all the blessings of creation.[4] The credo, in the sanctuary at the festival, is a daring polemical, political, defiant resolve to stake one's life on the truth of this narrative and on the reliability of the key character in the narrative. While the testimony of Israel may have captivated the children[5] and might have appealed to listening outsiders (as in Joshua 24),[6] the primary impact of such credo recital is undoubtedly upon those who themselves give utterance. Israel and its members are decisively defined by their public attestation of loyalty to YHWH that shapes their future. In the dramatic, covenantal sensibility of Israel, moreover, it is also thinkable that the recital had an impact upon and was in part designed to have an impact upon YHWH, reminding YHWH of ancient miracles as a model for miracles now urgently required by Israel.

There is in Israel a second, subordinate model of "credo recital," the Song of Thanksgiving. It is characteristic in Israel, according to the Psalms, that when one has been in need, has petitioned YHWH for help, and has received that help, to narrate the entire sequence of need, petition, and help. Claus Westermann has rightly termed those psalms "Narrative Psalms," for they tell in quite personal detail of miraculous rescue, a rescue that for the person involved is as overwhelming as was the Exodus for the larger narrative of Israel.[7] For example, in Psalm 30 the speaker tells about false confidence (v. 6), then about dismay (v. 7), supplication (vv. 8-9), petition (v. 10), and finally about the rescue of YHWH:

> You have turned my mourning into dancing;
>> you have taken off my sackcloth
>> and clothed me with joy,
> so that my soul may praise you and not be silent.

O LORD my God, I will give thanks to you forever.
(Ps 30:11-12)[8]

This same pattern is repeated four times in Psalm 107, wherein the speaker describes remembered peril and repentance, and then tells of rescue by YHWH that evokes testimony and thanks. The rescue stands at the center of the recital:

> And he delivered them from their distress;
> he led them by a straight way,
>> until they reached an inhabited town....
>> and he saved them from their distress;
> he brought them out of darkness and gloom,
>> and broke their bonds asunder....
>
>> and he saved them from their distress;
>
> he sent out his word and healed them,
>> and delivered them from destruction....
>> and he brought them out from their distress;
> he made the storm be still,
>> and the waves of the sea were hushed.
> (Pss 107: 6b-7, 13b-14, 19b-20, 28b-29; see Ps 116:1-9)

These modest, intimate statements are quite personal. They focus on personal moments of transformation and do not approximate in scope or force the great testimonies of the public credos. Nonetheless they are of the same genre that gives glad acclamation concerning inexplicable wonders that cannot be explained, but only attested. The substance and form of these *narrative Psalms* and of the *great credos* are quite parallel. It is, moreover, likely that those who offered such narrative accounts of personal transformation through divine intervention find these intimate attestations more powerful and more defining than the great public "miracles." Good pastoral worship of course does not choose between these two types of testimony, but gladly welcomes both the public manifestation of

YHWH and the personal attentiveness of this miracle-working God.

(2) Israel's most characteristic utterance in worship is *praise*, the exuberant rhetorical act of gladly ceding one's life and the life of the world over to YHWH in joyous self-abandonment.[9] Such praise is the concrete, bodily act of situating one's life in the power and presence of the one addressed, a willingness to hold nothing back for autonomous control, but a trustful submission to the other. This praise is a performed act whereby the one who sings (utters) enacts a self wholly given over to the other.

The recurring form of praise is in two parts. First, there is *a summons to praise* that consists in a vocative addressed to other members of the singing community, referring them to the one to whom the song of the community is to be directed.[10] Thus quite simply, "[You] Praise the LORD," or in Hebrew, *hallelu ... Yah* (Ps 117:1). The summons or invitation is forceful, but the accent is not on the vocative. It is on the name of the one to be praised, "Yah," or more fully "Yahweh." In the utterance of the name of the one to be praised, the singing community calls to mind and evokes all that the name entails of the blessing of creation and wonders of historical deliverance. As a result the name bespeaks the fullness of YHWH's character and the richness of YHWH's actions.

Very often the vocative is left unspecified and refers to the assembled congregation. But the vocative can be quite specific; the exuberance of the summons is given a sweeping expansiveness according to the company of those who are summoned. Thus the summons may be to "my soul" (Ps 146:1) or "Jerusalem, Zion" (Ps 147:12). The vocative may envision a mighty company in heaven and on earth:

> Bless the LORD, O you his angels,
>> you mighty ones who do his bidding,
>> obedient to his spoken word.
> Bless the LORD, all his hosts,
>> his ministers that do his will.

43

> Bless the LORD, all his works,
> in all places of his dominion.
> Bless the LORD, O my soul. (Ps 103:20-22)

It may be a detailed naming of "all creatures of our God and king" who are in glad, exuberant submission to the creator:

> Praise the LORD from the earth,
> you sea monsters and all deeps,
> fire and hail, snow and frost,
> stormy wind fulfilling his command! (Ps 148:7-8)

The fullness of the language attests to the splendor of the one addressed and the joyous passion of the one who speaks the imperative.

The second rhetorical element of praise, often introduced by the Hebrew particle *kî* ("for, because") consists in *reasons for praise.*[11] The reasons regularly given include either the character and attributes of YHWH or the remembered actions of YHWH. Most succinctly, the character of YHWH is summarized in Israel's most treasured words of reliability and fidelity:

> For great is his steadfast love toward us,
> and the faithfulness of the LORD endures forever.
> Praise the LORD! (Ps 117:2)

The terms "steadfast love" (*hesed*) and "faithfulness" (*'amunah*) summarize Israel's entire memory of miracles, and thus constitute a shorthand for the inventory that is more fully given in credo recital and in narrative psalms; conversely, the actions of YHWH bespeak YHWH's generous, generative power, both in creation and in historical processes:

> ... who made heaven and earth,
> the sea, and all that is in them;
> who keeps faith forever;
> who executes justice for the oppressed;

who gives food to the hungry.
The LORD sets the prisoners free;
   the LORD opens the eyes of the blind.
The LORD lifts up those who are bowed down;
   the LORD loves the righteous.
The LORD watches over the strangers;
   he upholds the orphan and the widow,
   but the way of the wicked he brings to ruin. (Ps 146:6-9)

It is clear that in reciting both *character and action*, the singing congregation describes, imagines, and evokes an alternative world in which YHWH's power for goodness and justice is known to be palpably efficacious. The singing is in order that the community may keep itself within this remarkable narrative that YHWH dominates.

The purpose of such praise, in the end, is "world construction."[12] To be sure, the primal impetus for doxology is that life has burst open beyond self and that bursting must be given voice. In the regular repeated action of praise, however, the community engages in an act of imagination that keeps the wondrous world of YHWH's good governance available and credible.

In a most primitive sense, such singing elevates or "magnifies" YHWH, that is, it makes God bigger. The impetus for such doxological action may be found in an assumption of polytheism in which YHWH is characteristically involved in a contest with other gods to see who would prevail. The claim of YHWH, understood most elementally, is powerfully enhanced by the loudness and vigor of Israel's singing. (Perhaps a rough analogy is the function of cheerleaders at sports events in which the supporting fans contribute to the force of "the team" by their loud enthusiasm.) This would seem to be reflected in the odd statement of Psalm 22:3: "Yet you are holy, enthroned on the praises of Israel." The imagery suggests that YHWH's throne rests upon Israel's doxologies. In such a figure, Israel can elevate YHWH above other gods by singing, so that YHWH is more prominent, more visible, and more enhanced than the other gods. Everything thus depends for God's cause upon the singing of the community.

The imaginative quality of praise serves to generate a "world" of covenantal possibility that is presided over by a good, powerful, attentive, holy covenant partner. In the first instant, such singing serves to describe such a world that is known to be true. In the emotive experience of the congregation, however, such communal singing not only describes, but summons and evokes such a "world." Consequently, the assembly can depart the meeting with a new certitude that this "world" is indeed ruled by One who can be trusted and that warrants serious allegiance.

As the world is secured through the celebration (and the enthronement) of YHWH, doxology also has a polemical function of denying, refusing, and eventually deconstructing other worlds that are incompatible with the rule of YHWH. Thus in that ancient world, to say "praise YHWH" quite concretely implied the negative, "and not Baal, not Dagon, not Marduk." In our contemporary world, doxologies toward this God may variously constitute a rejection of a world of greed, anxiety, and violence, a world of technological manipulation or of therapeutic deception or of romantic autonomy. The character of YHWH at the center of doxology emboldens the worshiping community to resist, in quite specific and deliberate ways, the powers of death that are intimately present and disastrously seductive among us.[13] When the worshiping congregation falls out of the world of the doxology (by absenting itself from praise), moreover, it becomes a ready candidate for other worlds over which YHWH does not preside and in which the gifts of life are not on offer from YHWH.

(3) Israel's speech in worship was not all-exuberant worship, grateful remembering, and affirmation of YHWH. As a counterpoint to such affirmation in credo and doxology, Israel also engaged in *truth-telling* about its life with YHWH in confession,

lament, and protest. This feature of Israel's rhetoric is a most decisive mark of Israel's worship. It indicates that in worship as a covenantal transaction Israel was not a submissive, second-rate player, but was a full, vigorous partner to YHWH with an unapologetic presence and an unembarrassed voice that refused to be silenced or cowed. As this practice of speech is a crucial mark of Israel's worship, so it is also a dimension of worship that has been largely lost in much of church practice that is by contrast with Israel's worship, one-sidedly submissive.[14] Israel refuses to submit too readily to YHWH's sovereignty when that sovereignty was seen to be unfaithful; in such circumstances, Israel instead of submitting, made a claim for itself against YHWH. Israel insisted, in highly stylized liturgic cadences, not only that YHWH had important covenantal obligations to Israel, but that YHWH had, much too often, failed in those obligations.

(a) Israel's candid truth-telling in worship readily declares before YHWH its own *guilt and failure to honor covenant.* This element of Israel's speech is readily recognized in the Christian practice of "confession of sin." This dimension of truth-telling is expressed in the so-called "Pauline Psalms" (Pss 6, 32, 38, 51, 102, 130, 143), of which the best known is Psalm 51:

> For I know my transgressions,
>   and my sin is ever before me.
> Against you, you alone, have I sinned,
>   and done what is evil in your sight,
> so that you are justified in your sentence
>   and blameless when you pass judgment.
> Indeed, I was born guilty,
>   a sinner when my mother conceived me. (Ps 51:3-5)

Israel, here in the mouth of David, acknowledges its failure and seeks forgiveness from YHWH. Such a notion, however, should not be overstated either in the frequency of such references or in the primacy of such confession to Israel. Fredrik Lindström has meticulously shown that the individual Psalms of Lament

characteristically do not dwell on such failure and guilt.[15] They
tell of deep trouble; they do not, however, entertain the thought
that trouble comes as warranted punishment. We may juxtapose
this lack of such an accent to the priestly rituals of purgation and
purification. We may conclude that Israel had sufficient confidence in such sacramental practices that it did not need to be preoccupied with failure, the sort of preoccupation that became
much more central in "the introspective conscience of the West."[16]

(b) Israel's candid truth-telling in worship did not linger over
guilt and failure, but much more focused on *loss and sadness* and
the sense of its own *helplessness* before trouble. Such weary
helplessness is evident in such articulations attributed to
"Zion" in Jeremiah 8:19-20 and Isaiah 49:14, the latter being
apparently a quote from the liturgical text of Lamentations 5:20.
The book of Lamentations, as Kathleen O'Connor has seen,
articulates the tears of Jerusalem, the tears of Israel, and eventually "the tears of the world."[17] While there are some acknowledgments of guilt in that text, that is not the accent point.
Rather, the tone is one of deep loss and profound grief, the exilic reality of having "none to comfort" (Lam 1:2, 9, 17, and 21):

> She weeps bitterly in the night,
>   with tears on her cheeks;
> among all her lovers
>   she has no one to comfort her;
> all her friends have dealt treacherously with her,
>   they have become her enemies. (Lam 1:2)

While there is acknowledgement of guilt (as in 3:42), the culmi-
nation of such a thought is rather,

> Those who were my enemies without cause
>   have hunted me like a bird;
> they flung me alive into a pit
>   and hurled stones on me;
> water closed over my head;
>   I said, "I am lost." (Lam 3:52-54)

It is this suffering "without cause" that leads to the glad conclusion that YHWH has heard Israel's petition and has responded with "fear not" (3:57).

(c) Beyond *guilt* and *sadness* marked by *helplessness*, however, Israel's candid truth-telling in worship articulates *rage* at the undeserved, unbearable situation of social shame, rejection, and suffering. In these lament psalms, Israel speaks a voice of indignation that refuses to accept such suffering and knows very well that such suffering is unwarranted. Such speech, in its rawness, is in fact an expression of great faith; it expresses deep conviction that when YHWH is mobilized in order to honor YHWH's covenantal commitments to Israel, YHWH has full power and capacity to right any situation of wrong. Thus the voice of protest and rage is characteristically in the service of plea and petition to YHWH.

Israel's rage is articulated against those who abuse; Israel seeks YHWH's vengeance against the enemy. The "enemy" in these speeches may be variously "the wicked" within the community, or a foreign enemy, or simply an unnamed and unspecified foe.[18] In any case Israel seeks vengeance and asks YHWH to act to transform an unbearable situation and to deal decisively with the perpetrators of such suffering:

Rise up, O LORD!
    Deliver me, O my God!
For you strike all my enemies on the cheek;
    you break the teeth of the wicked. (Ps 3:7)

* * *

The boastful will not stand before your eyes;
    you hate all evildoers.
You destroy those who speak lies;
    the LORD abhors the bloodthirsty and deceitful. (Ps 5:5-6)

* * *

Break the arm of the wicked and evildoers;
    seek out their wickedness until you find none.

49

> The LORD is king forever and ever;
> the nations shall perish from his land. (Ps 10:15-16)

Such rhetoric, unpalatable as it is in the piety of conventional Christianity, is in fact a bold claim for justice and well-being to which YHWH's people are entitled.[19] Such rhetoric of violence, moreover, in fact submits the thirst for violence to YHWH as an alternative to taking vengeance into one's own hands. Israel knows that "vengeance is mine," that only YHWH can rightly recompense, and so Israel makes a bid for YHWH's action (Deut 32:35; Rom 12:19).[20] Such rhetoric of course is absent in most Christian worship. Such an absence, in this judgment, needs to be reconsidered because the failure to acknowledge and express such a hunger for retaliation—that is surely present in every congregation—is an invitation to denial.[21] As a result, legitimate indignation is regularly siphoned away from speech with God to be acted out in other, perhaps more destructive ways. Such speech of rage addressed to YHWH is credible only when the worshiping community has confidence that the covenant God addressed is both willing and able to intervene in contexts of unbearable suffering. It may be noted that bourgeoisie worship in the settled West looks askance at such rhetoric, but in disordered societies in other parts of the world, such speech of protest and insistence is credible and pervasive.[22]

Beyond rage addressed to YHWH concerning enemies who need to be punished, however, the daring truth-telling speech of Israel in worship goes even further to voice the conviction that YHWH in YHWH's own self has reneged on covenantal obligation. YHWH, it is asserted, is an unreliable, even destructive partner.[23] This shrill voice of protest against divine infidelity exhibits Israel's liturgical willingness to claim its own right before YHWH, even at YHWH's expense. There are, to be sure, not so many texts of this kind; in the church in an increasingly brutalizing world, however, the recovery of these texts is surely important. Thus Israel can protest against YHWH's silence and failure to answer Israel's cry of need:

50

O LORD, God of my salvation,
> when, at night, I cry out in your presence,
let my prayer come before you;
> incline your ear to my cry....
Every day I call on you, O LORD;
> I spread out my hands to you....
But I, O LORD, cry out to you;
> in the morning my prayer comes before you. (Ps 88:1-2, 9*b*, 13)

YHWH had promised to be attentive to Israel (see, for example, Isa 58:9; 65:24), but Israel knows about divine silence that makes the world unbearable and the suffering nonsensical.[24] Beyond silence, however, Israel can accuse YHWH of having initiated the suffering of Israel. Psalm 44, in anticipation of Job's protests, carried the accusation directly to "You":[25]

Yet you have rejected us and abased us,
> and have not gone out with our armies.
You made us turn back from the foe,
> and our enemies have gotten spoil.
> You have made us like sheep for slaughter,
> and have scattered us among the nations.
You have sold your people for a trifle,
> demanding no high price for them.
You have made us the taunt of our neighbors,
> the derision and scorn of those around us.
You have made us a byword among the nations,
> a laughingstock among the peoples.
All day long my disgrace is before me,
> and shame has covered my face
at the words of the taunters and revilers,
> at the sight of the enemy and the avenger.
All this has come upon us,
> yet we have not forgotten you,
> or been false to your covenant.
Our heart has not turned back,
> nor have our steps departed from your way,

51

> yet you have broken us in the haunt of jackals,
>> and covered us with deep darkness. (Ps 44:9-19)

It is clear that in such daring speech, Israel pushes to the limit the capacity for covenant dialogue. The wonder of Israel's liturgical daring is that such utterance not only was sounded, but it entered Israel's "hymnal." The further wonder is that such speech did not cause termination of the covenant but, rather, as Israel anticipated, led to new divine initiative. The petition of Psalm 44:23-26 indicates that such vigorous protest was not a dismissal of YHWH, but in fact a ground for YHWH's new initiative:

> Rouse yourself! Why do you sleep, O Lord?
>> Awake, do not cast us off forever!
> Why do you hide your face?
>> Why do you forget our affliction and oppression?
> For we sink down to the dust;
>> our bodies cling to the ground.
> Rise up, come to our help.
>> Redeem us for the sake of your steadfast love. (Ps 44:23-26)

In its profound suffering and humiliation, Israel makes use of the most affrontive rhetoric to mobilize YHWH. In the sum of Israel's prayers, we are led to believe that such prayer is not an act of unfaith, but rather is the supreme example of serious faith. More than that, Israel is convinced, utterly convinced, that such speech will cause new divine initiative. It is such conviction that causes Israel to utter such speech. There is savage interactive realism in this conversation that depends upon a post-critical "second naiveté" about YHWH.[26] In its worship, Israel never doubted the legitimacy or the effectiveness of such rhetoric. Such daring, abrasive utterances stand alongside Israel's glad credos of affirmation and Israel's exuberant doxologies addressed to YHWH. Neither cancels out the other mode of speech. This full, rich relationship requires utterance in more than one genre.

In the end, this rich rhetorical practice that voices hurt and hope in extremity amounts to petition.[27] The petition to Yhwh can be explicit or only implied. Either way, the utterance of Israel is designed to move YHWH to intervention in full confidence of YHWH's capacity for effective intervention. Such petition, for all the savage rhetoric, is Israel's acknowledgment of dependence upon YHWH, and YHWH's capacity for rescue. The mood of the whole is one of covenantal confidence.[28] In such speech Israel has a sense of its own entitlement and is resolved to require of YHWH that to which Israel in covenant is entitled.[29]

The gestures of worship in Israel (festivals, sacrifices) seem largely to have been borrowed from Canaanite cultic practice and participate in a common cultural practice. The utterances of worship in Israel (speeches of YHWH who commands, guides, and assures; the speeches of Israel who confesses, praises, and laments), by contrast, are quite specific to the covenantal relationship between these two partners. Finally, I want to reflect upon the relationship of gesture and utterance in order to suggest that utterances also claim gestures as specific to this relationship. In context, the gestures are no longer defined in generically cultural ways. While the convergence of gesture and utterance may be found in many places in Israel's life, here I reflect upon the convergence in Israel's act of thanksgiving to YHWH that must have been central to its worship.

Thanksgiving (Hebrew *tôdah*) in Israel was a passionate, generous, public response to YHWH for YHWH's gift or action that impinged upon the life of Israel in positive and decisive ways. It may be occasional and ad hoc, and certainly is in response to some matter that is quite concrete. Nonetheless, it is a response to YHWH that is highly stylized and that is understood as part—as the culminating part—of the larger narrative interaction between YHWH and Israel:

No hymn was more familiar in Israel and none more frequently sung than the song of thanksgiving celebrating the divine goodness (Ps 136; cf. Pss 106:1; 107:1; 118:1; 135:3; 2 Chron 7:3).[30]

Specifically, the *tôdah* is twinned to and is to be understood as the completion of petition. Thus Israel asks YHWH for relief; when relief is given, Israel offers to YHWH in response a glad *tôdah*. In the *tôdah* Israel characteristically reiterates the initial trouble and the initial petition to which YHWH has given answer. The petition and the *tôdah* are, moreover, bound together by a vow. Thus while in trouble, Israel may make a vow to YHWH to bring an offering when deliverance is enacted (1 Sam 1:11; Pss 7:17; 65:1-2). And then, faithful to the initial pledge, the recipient of goodness pays the promised vow to YHWH who has answered the petition (Pss 22:25; 116:14).

The act of *tôdah* is clearly a *concrete, material gesture* that constitutes an act of worship, an act of devotion and loyalty to YHWH. Thus the thank offering is specified in the inventory of sacrifices in Leviticus 7:11-15 wherein the detail of the procedure is provided (see Lev 22:29 as well). The offering of something of value, variously animal or grain offering, is a public acknowledgment of loyalty to YHWH. Characteristically, however, the provision, in the presentation of Leviticus, offers no words, only prescribed actions.

We do, however, have the words that accompany the act in other texts, wherein it is clear that gesture and utterance come together; thank offering requires and permits both act and speech. As elsewhere, it is the speech that gives the act specificity and that positions the act as a covenantal transaction between YHWH and Israel. Thank offerings of act and speech recur in Israel's narrative account of its life with YHWH (see Exod 18:12; Jonah 2:1-10; 2 Chr 30:21-22). It is in the Psalms, however, that we find the most direct evidence for this speech/act that so richly characterizes Israel's worship. Psalm 30 narrates and celebrates a quite personal deliverance, vows to "give thanks to you forever," and invites the congregation of the "faithful ones" to "give thanks to his holy name" (vv. 4, 12). In Psalm 40, the speaker is jubilant about deliverance (vv. 1-3) and bears witness to the congregation:

I have told the glad news of deliverance
     in the great congregation;
see, I have not restrained my lips,
     as you know, O LORD.
I have not hidden your saving
     help within my heart,
I have spoken of your
     faithfulness and your salvation;
I have not concealed your steadfast love and your faithfulness
     from the great congregation. (Ps 40:9-10)

In Psalm 66, the speaker celebrates YHWH's awesome deeds (v. 5). The action of thanks is reported in verses 13-15:

I will come into your house with burnt offerings;
     I will pay you my vows,
those that my lips uttered
     and my mouth promised when I was in trouble.
I will offer to you burnt offerings of fatlings,
     with the smoke of the sacrifice of rams;
I will make an offering of bulls and goats. (Ps 66:13-15)

Speech accompanies the act of thanks in verses 16-19:

Come and hear, all you who fear God,
     and I will tell what he has done for me.
I cried aloud to him,
     and he was extolled with my tongue.
If I had cherished iniquity in my heart,
     the Lord would not have listened.
But truly God has listened;
     he has given heed to the words of my prayer. (Ps 66:16-19)

In Psalm 116, the speaker articulates the rescue wrought by YHWH (vv. 5-10), and then presents a thank offering:

> I will lift up the cup of salvation
>> and call on the name of the LORD,
> I will pay my vows to the LORD
>> in the presence of all his people.
> Precious in the sight of the LORD
>> is the death of his faithful ones.
> O LORD, I am your servant;
>> I am your servant, the child of your serving girl.
>> You have loosed my bonds.
> I will offer to you a thanksgiving sacrifice
>> and call on the name of the LORD.
> I will pay my vows to the LORD
>> in the presence of all his people,
> in the courts of the house of the LORD,
>> in your midst, O Jerusalem.
> Praise the LORD! (Ps 116:13-19)

Psalm 118 celebrates a victory and is saturated with thanks. It begins (v. 1) and ends (v. 29) with a conventional formula of thanks. The same motif swirls in what is clearly a liturgical context in verses 19, 21, 28; and in verse 17, the psalm suggests words that accompany the cultic act: "I shall not die, but I shall live, and recount the deeds of the LORD" (Ps 118:17). We may mention two texts in particular that concern thank offerings. In Psalm 107, the recital of thanks enumerates four characteristic cases of rescue for which testimony is given: desert sojourn (vv. 4-9), prison (vv. 10-16), sickness (vv. 17-22), and storm at sea (vv. 23-32). In each highly stylized case, the speaker reports the trouble and the petition addressed to YHWH. And then the speaker in each case attests to YHWH's rescue. The attestation does not, however, end with such an affirmation; it continues in order to invite thanks to YHWH: "Let them thank the LORD for his steadfast love" (vv. 8, 15, 21, 31). We may, moreover, notice two decisive variations in the formula. In verse 22, in the third scenario, the summons to testimony continues: "And let them offer thanksgiving sacrifices, and tell of his deeds with songs of joy" (v. 22). In this summons to act, sacrifice and the utterance are combined. In verse 32, moreover, this summons continues as an invitation to the congregation to join the praise: "Let them extol him in the congregation of the people, and praise him in the assembly of the elders" (v. 32). Clearly, act and word are together evoked, as Israel must give verbal, material expression to its amazement and gratitude concerning new life from YHWH that it could not secure for itself. Westermann comments on such a response after rescue that may take the form of a payment of vow:

> Such a vow in the midst of affliction is grossly misunderstood if we interpret it as a deal with God according to the motto: "If you give me this, I will give you that." Rather, it expresses the fact that the association between him who prays to God and God is not to come to an end when God has rescued him, but that after rescue it will continue in this, that he who has been rescued will tell his brothers about the rescue he experienced.[31]

Finally, attention should be paid to the recital in Deuteronomy 26:5-9, Gerhard von Rad's famous credo.[32] This recital, a typical stylized summary of Israel's salvific memory, is set exactly in a context of worship. Given the familiar account of the recital, it is not so often noticed that the recital is set in a sanctuary, before a priest, together with an offering of "the first of all the fruit of the ground." The "first fruit of the ground" refers to the blessings of agriculture, but in Israel's practice that blessing from the land is tied to the promise of the land and consequently to "YHWH's mighty deeds."

All of these texts evidence that Israel had a regular liturgical procedure whereby it gave public, dramatic testimony that its life and well-being were free gifts of YHWH who responded attentively and powerfully to Israel's need. The act of thanks is public and material. It likely entailed a meal (see Exod 18:12; 2 Chr 30:21-22; Ps 22:26), and it certainly involved the entire congregation (Pss 22:23-26; 40:10-11; 66:16; 116:14). The incident evoking gratitude may be personal and intimate. But the depth of gratitude felt required that the gratitude go public, to gather the entire community in expressions of thanks; the particular occasion of thanks is thereby transposed into a great jubilee event of solidarity, joy, and well-being, as Israel characteristically extrapolates great theological claims from the concreteness of its life. In such an extrapolation, the specificity of thanks shades over into the more generic exuberance and celebration of praise. It remains rooted, however, in the concreteness of life transformed.

While the worship of Israel, in act and in word, is complex and variegated, we may provisionally suggest that in the end thanks is the primal ingredient in Israel's worship. It is a *bodily, verbal, public* declaration that life is a gift and that all of life, in Israel and in all creation, is gladly dependent upon and derived from Yhwh's extravagant, generous, reliable self-giving. While evidence abounds in this direction, the point is not self-evident or beyond dispute. Claus Westermann, the most acute psalm scholar of his generation, has expressed deep reservation that thanks can be distinguished from praise, and that if it can be distinguished, it is a lesser quality theological claim. He takes a quite minimalist view of thanks through the following propositions:[33]

1. In praise the one being praised is elevated ... in thanks the one thanked remains in place.

2. In praise I am directed entirely toward the one whom I praise, and this means, of necessity, in that moment a looking away from myself. In thanks I am expressing *my* thanks.

3. Freedom and spontaneity belong to the essence of praise; giving thanks can become a duty.

4. Praise has a forum and always occurs in a group; giving thanks is private, for it need concern no one except the one thanking and the one being thanked.

5. Praise is essentially joyful; giving thanks can take on the character of something required. Praise can never, but thanks must often, be commanded.

6. The most important verbal mark of difference is that thanking occurs in the speaking of the words, "thank you," or in a shortened form, "thanks"; genuine spontaneous praise occurs in a sentence in which the one being praised is the subject, "thou hast done," or "thou art...."

Miller has provided a careful critique of Westermann's view.[34] It is clear that Westermann fears that thanks is excessively a *quid pro quo* that detracts from the singularity of YHWH. But such an interaction as thanks is exactly appropriate to a relationship that is intensely covenantal and zealously dialogical.

Thus against Westermann, the free act and voice of gratitude acknowledge the blessings of the creator and the rescues of the redeemer. Harvey Guthrie, by way of contrast with the position of Westermann, has explored the way in which *tôdah* is the taproot of a theological-liturgical tradition that has culminated, for Christians, in the Eucharist, which is in the words of my own liturgical tradition, "the innermost sanctuary of the whole Christian worship."[35] Harmut Gese suggests that the Eucharist is to be understood as related to the meal that is evidenced in Psalm 22:26 and is a case of the thank offering:

> With the supper that instituted fellowship and a New Being, there must inseparably be associated the praise of Yahweh, the acknowledgement of Yahweh as the rescuer by means of the memorial of the saving event...the Lord's Supper deals with the *tôdah* of the Risen One.[36]

Guthrie makes the argument that praise (so championed by Westermann) characteristically arises in the great cult of the state, whereas thanks arises in the midst of social contexts where the very gift of daily bread is received and appreciated.[37] Thus thanks, in word and act, becomes the hallmark of

Christian worship in traditions as broad as Benedictine and Calvinist practice. Such practice tells against every easy self-help temptation in an ancient religious environment of superstition and magical manipulation. It offers a simple assertion of the free gift of YHWH by which life comes. Thanks is no less crucial in the contemporary world of self-making and self-securing; that thanks is an intensely evangelical practice of affirmation and reference of all life to the God who gives it. The very sustenance of life is voiced on the lips of the pastor who can say, "The gifts of God for the people of God." The congregation can respond:

> Now thank we all our God, with hearts and hands and voices,
> who wondrous things has done, in whom this world rejoices;
> who from our mothers' arms has blest us on our way
> with countless gifts of love, and still is ours today.[38]

Before the congregation departs the meal of thanks, its last word in Eucharist is a prayer of thanksgiving:

> Almighty and everliving God, we most heartily thank thee for that thou dost feed us, in these holy mysteries, with the spiritual food of the most precious Body and Blood of thy Son our Savior Jesus Christ; and does assure us thereby of thy favor and goodness toward us; and that we are very members incorporate in the mystical body of thy Son, the blessed company of all faithful people; and are also heirs through hope, of thy everlasting kingdom.[39]

In this response the people of God, in act and in word, do the deed that is most constitutive of life, a gesture rooted deep and intensely counter-cultural in a technological world that wants not to believe in gift. I will leave the last word on this wondrous response to divine generosity to my teacher:

> We are now prepared to understand why it is "good" for Israel to worship God. It is good because in worship she has

60

discerned the source of her existence and the destiny to which she is called. It is good because her historical life is ordered and steadied by the rule of a transcendent Lord. It is good because in the cult she hears the word of forgiveness. It is good because behind and within her life there is an ultimate love which comprehends all, judges in terrible wrath, and yet is merciful. This is why Israel can praise God even for his judgment upon her.... In her worship, Israel realizes that she is free from the slaveries which enslave the hearts of men.... For in the hymns, laments, confessions, thanksgivings, songs of trust, and blessings, we are listening to the words of released and liberated men. In the sanctuary, these men are free to speak, free to pray, free to confess their sins, free to disclose the awful secrets of the heart, free... to call out in almost blasphemous cries, but also free to sing and praise and adore, and in this last freedom they are free indeed, for they have been delivered from the egocentricities and self-obsessions which lay men low and make them trivial and caviling.

It is not surprising, therefore, that as the Psalter draws to a close the sound of singing grows ever more triumphant and joyous. These men of Israel are praising God that he alone is God and that the gods of the nations are but idols.[40]

CHAPTER 5

Worship: Israel at "Play"

In this final discussion, I will consider seven dimensions of indeterminacy that operate in Israel's worship, and that characterize the covenantal transaction that takes place between YHWH and Israel in Israel's worship. By "play" in the title of this chapter, I do not refer to "play" in the sense of entertainment, leisure, frivolity, or devil-may-care unbridled self-expression.[1] Rather, I refer to "play" as the slippage that we call "play" in the turning of a steering wheel on a car.[2] I use the term to indicate that while Israel's worship is exclusive between the two parties of the covenant, it consists in interaction that is thick, freighted, laden with alternative possibilities, and open to a kind of ambiguity that respects the integrity and freedom of both parties. To that extent, it is a practice that is to some great extent indeterminate, that is, still to be determined, and therefore unsettled; it must, moreover, remain to some extent unsettled, given the nature of the transaction and the characters who are "at play" together in worship. I mean to suggest that worship that is excessively "determined"—by dogmatic certitude, by moralistic zeal, or any other mode of excessive closure—distorts a relationship that is inescapably

63

fraught with risk, passion, and freedom; this is a relationship that claims the whole attention of both parties. Any attempt to order worship in a way that minimizes these qualities misconstrues the character of Israel's worship and the God worshiped by Israel. Thematic articulations of this "play" include the following:

(1) *The play of obedience and freedom.* There is no doubt that the worship of Israel, rooted in Sinai, concerns exclusive loyalty to YHWH that is grounded in and informed by commandments to which Israel has sworn allegiance (Exod 24:3, 7). The first two commands of Sinai—"...no other gods...no graven images"— define that exclusivism (Exod 20:3-6).[3] It is this radical, uncompromising summons to obedience that causes the tradition informed by Deuteronomy to be saturated with the verb "listen" *(shama')*, rooted in the *"shema'"* of Deuteronomy 6:4-5:

> Hear, O Israel: The LORD is our God, the LORD alone. You shall love the LORD your God with all your heart, and with all your soul, and with all your might.

It is this same radical, uncompromising summons to obedience that issues, in the Priestly tradition, in a requirement of holiness like unto the holiness of YHWH: "You shall be holy, for I the LORD your God am holy" (Lev 19:2b). Israel's raison d'être, practiced in worship as in life, is to submit to the character and purpose of YHWH by obeying the commands of Sinai.

It would be a mistake, however, to imagine that Israel's worship is an act of simple, absolute, one-dimensional obedience such as zealots sometimes try to make it. To the contrary, Israel's life with YHWH—and consequently Israel's practice of worship—is indeed a function of freedom in the zone of freedom assured by a covenantal relationship of freedom.[4] That relationship is complex and variegated, and Israel at worship engaged the full range of that complexity.

We may cite two unmistakable evidences of worship as an act

of freedom. First, the proclamation of Torah as divine will was a central preoccupation of worship, a preoccupation that eventuated in the "sermon" as explication. We have already noted the immense act of interpretation that Torah proclamation evoked in Deuteronomy 1:5 and Nehemiah 8:7-8.[5] Further, the enormous amount of material generated in Torah instruction in the Priestly and Deuteronomic traditions, echoed respectively in Ezekiel and Jeremiah, fully exhibits emancipated imagination in the interpretive act whereby Torah is kept enduringly contemporary. It is clear that the act of proclamation and interpretation of Torah is no flat, one-dimensional enterprise; it is rather a work of free covenant partners fully capable of and authorized to take great imaginative leaps of interpretation that are possible only in freedom. These Torah interpreters did not cringe in fear before that task, but brought to their work of obedience all of the liberty that belongs to covenant.

Second, the laments, complaints, and protests we have noted above—particularly modeled in the prayers of Moses in Exodus 32:11-14, 33:15-16, Numbers 11:11-15 and 14:13-19—exhibit no flat submissiveness to YHWH.[6] Rather these prayers exhibit an immense and nervy freedom to stand with and stand before and stand over against YHWH in covenant that is conducted in freedom. The *requirement of obedience* in worship and the *practice of freedom* in worship together constitute an ongoing reality in Israel's life.[7] Care must be taken not to eliminate the "play" of this tension that keeps the transition open, vibrant, serious, and demanding.

(2) *The play of holiness and justice.* There is no doubt that the worship of Israel—with its holy priests, holy festivals, holy diets, holy places—was designed to create a community of holiness, of purity and cleanness, that is fully devoted to life in the Holy Presence of YHWH.[8] The establishment and maintenance of such a symmetrical and ordered zone of holiness in which Israel's life is situated is the evident purpose of the Priestly tradition.[9] This agenda, moreover, is not limited to the Priestly

tradition for, as Norbert Lohfink has seen, even Deuteronomy has an agenda of holiness (Deut 7:6; 14:2, 21; 26:19).[10] Lohfink has made clear, however, the holiness enjoined in Deuteronomy is not confined to the cult (as with the Priestly tradition). It is, rather, a quite innovative form of holiness that concerns the creation of a *holy people* in a *holy land*. It is evident that the agenda of Deuteronomy moves outside the cultic zone of holiness envisioned by the Priestly tradition. As it does so, moreover, the zeal for holiness shades over into issues of justice; Deuteronomy is preoccupied with care for the poor and the marginated in a way that calls for a very different notion of holiness, a holiness that is expressed as compassion and economic transformation in order to create a new bond between "haves and have-nots."[11] This move from *holiness* toward *justice* is a primary interpretive maneuver in the tradition of Deuteronomy. That interpretive practice, however, is not limited to Deuteronomy; it is clear that even in the Priestly tradition, so preoccupied with "right ordering," the horizon of social justice is operative. As we have seen, even in the festival calendar of Leviticus 23:22, the sequence of festivals is turned toward care for the poor. Beyond that, Mary Douglas has shown how Leviticus 18 and 20, two texts now much accented in church disputes, function as a frame for Leviticus 19.[12] In that text "neighbor love" is enjoined (Lev 19:19), and it is urged that there must be equity for the poor and the alien, without reference to any holiness regulation:

> You shall not render an unjust judgment; you shall not be partial to the poor or defer to the great: with justice you shall judge your neighbor. (Lev 19:15)
>
> *   *   *
>
> When an alien resides with you in your land, you shall not oppress the alien. The alien who resides with you shall be to you as the citizen among you; you shall love the alien as yourself, for you were aliens in the land of Egypt: I am the LORD your God. (Lev 19:33-34)

Of course it is in Leviticus 25 that the great teaching on the Jubilee year occurs that is designed to maintain the integrity of land and community.[13] The provision for Jubilee is to be understood as an agendum of holiness that reaches toward justice: "For it is a jubilee; it shall be holy to you: you shall eat only what the field itself produces" (Lev 25:12).

The tension is acute and ongoing in Israel between a worship community that keeps itself pure without respect to its social environment and a worship community that lets its practice spill over into the world of political, economic reality. Both practices are there in the worship tradition of Israel, deeply intertwined in the two great interpretive traditions of the priests and the Deuteronomists. This tension is now of immense importance in the contemporary church, for we have arrived at a disputatious place where church leaders and people want to choose sides concerning either *holiness* or *justice*. Would that it were so easy or so obvious! But it is not; Israel must endlessly renegotiate the matter in its practice.

A concern for holiness without reference to justice becomes ghettoized and turned in on itself in a static way. A concern for justice without reference to holiness becomes easily cut off from the sovereign God who makes all social strategies penultimate. A church faithful to these worship traditions must, in this judgment, do the more difficult task of letting *zeal for holiness* and *passion for justice* correct each other, thus keeping either accent from becoming absolute and so resistant to the reality of YHWH who stands before and behind all such urgent mandates. Care must be taken not to eliminate the "play" of this tension that prevents worship from being preempted by any particular preferred ideological conviction.

(3) *The play of state cult and the worship of family and clan.* Until recently, Old Testament worship was treated in scholarly discussion as an undifferentiated whole that reflected the force of the Jerusalem Temple. While there is no doubt of the preeminence of the Temple in Israel's worship, recent social scientific

investigation has been able to make important sociological differentiations that issue in quite different theological convictions and religious practices. Largely through the work of Rainer Albertz and Erhard Gerstenberger, it is now clear that family, clan, and tribe conducted worship of YHWH alongside the state cult in Jerusalem.[14] Sometimes these practices overlapped or were even integrated in the tradition; each, however, made its own articulation, a fact that requires our interpretive practice to attend to the complexity and richness of the whole.

There is no doubt that the liturgic practice of the Jerusalem Temple, sponsored by the Davidic dynasty, dominated the imagination of those who generated the Old Testament, a fact that is evident in the book of Psalms. The theological enterprise of Jerusalem, so much informed by and indebted to the claims of state religion, appealed to the great cosmological myths of creation, and offered a vision of the creator God as guarantor of Jerusalem.[15] At the same time, this liturgic enterprise vouched for the pivotal and defining role of the Davidic king in the delivery and maintenance of God-given cosmic order with political and economic concreteness.[16] This connection is evident in the so-called "Royal Psalms" that celebrate this crucial and distinctive role of the Davidic king in the great visionary promises of YHWH.[17] This liturgic tradition bore witness to the wonder of the creator God who is given nuance in liturgic rhetoric as warrior, king, and judge.[18] The importance of this large vision of YHWH, committed to the Davidic dynasty and to the holy city, was to proffer legitimacy for the regime and for the people linked to the regime. Thus Israel, in Temple worship, could rest its life in the large sovereign power of the God who would uphold the establishment in justice and who would uphold the world in righteousness and equity:

> God is our refuge and strength,
> > a very present help in trouble.
> Therefore we will not fear, though the earth should change,
> > though the mountains shake in the heart of the sea;

though its waters roar and foam,
> though the mountains tremble with its tumult....

The LORD of hosts is with us;
> the God of Jacob is our refuge. (Ps 46:1-3, 7)

*   *   *

Say among the nations, "The LORD is king!
> The world is firmly established; it shall never be moved.
> He will judge the peoples with equity."

Then shall all the trees of the forest sing for joy
> before the LORD; for he is coming,
> for he is coming to judge the earth.

He will judge the world with righteousness,
> and the peoples with his truth. (Ps 96:10, 12*b*)

Alongside that great liturgic enterprise, in more local and domestic settings, the subcommunities of Israel practiced worship that was attuned to the dailyness of life and to the rhythms of birth and death, of gift and loss on an intimate scale, rhythms of which the great temple liturgy took no special note.[19] This mode of worship featured a particular intimacy between YHWH and the worshiper. It is in this world that personal prayers of petition were uttered and in this world that the congregation was invited to join the petitioner in giving thanks in the wake of prayer answered. Gerstenberger goes so far as to suggest that the God known in such worship is one of intimacy and compassion, one not imagined in the state metaphors of warrior, judge, and king. Out of that discussion, Gerstenberger draws the theological judgment that such a God may be known to be in solidarity with those who suffer, but perhaps not strong enough to effect transformative change.[20] It is clear that such a subcommunity would provide a quite alternative testimony to YHWH.

There is no doubt of the sociological differentiations that produced enormously differentiated theological affirmations. The importance of those differentiations is that they remind us that theological testimony in the Bible, especially as pertains to worship, is variegated in sharp and crucial ways. Such an awareness warns against a reductionism to which the church is often tempted. On the one hand, in the interest of great public justice or in the interest of national, patriotic causes, it is tempting to take the truth of the state liturgy of Jerusalem as the only evidence of liturgy, a seduction to which Old Testament study has often succumbed. On the other hand, the church, since the rationalistic preemptions of the Enlightenment, has been tempted to retreat from the public domain and to settle for a God who is concerned for bourgeoisie "family values."

Against the first temptation, this spectrum of testimony in the Old Testament reminds us that the concreteness of suffering to which the familial God responds precludes singular focus upon the great public issues of order, justice, and legitimacy.[21] Conversely against the second temptation, this spectrum of testimony makes clear that exclusive focus on the familial and the local to the neglect of the great public issues in worship is untenable. The tension reminds us that every theological claim that arises out of sociological circumstance is context specific. No single theological advocacy can be given interpretive hegemony, even if the context and testimony preferred is that of the most powerful. Care must be taken not to eliminate the "play" of this tension that precludes a sociological-theological reductionism. Such a reductionism restricts the wonder of this God and the requirements of worship that are congruent with the richness of YHWH's character.

(4) *The play of Torah and king.* Among the most prominent tensions in recent Old Testament theology is that between the covenantal traditions of Torah championed by the Deuteronomists and the promises of YHWH made to David and to the Davidic dynasty. The Torah traditions of Sinai, relentlessly pursued by the Deuteronomists, makes obedience to Torah the non-negotiable condition of covenant with YHWH. Thus already in Exodus 19:5, this tradition places a great "If" at the base of Israel's life with YHWH. This conditionality for life in

covenant is carried through the Deuteronomic literature, as for example 1 Kings 3:14; 6:12; 9:4-6. YHWH's commitment to David, however, is a refusal of such a powerful program of *quid pro quo*, for the commitment of YHWH to David and to David's house is, in the end, beyond any condition: "But I will not take my steadfast love from him, as I took it from Saul, whom I put away from before you" (2 Sam 7:15).

These two theological accents move in very different directions. Von Rad has shown the way in which the Deuteronomic historian in 1 and 2 Kings has managed, as best that could be done, to hold the two together in something of an interpretive coherence.[22] Before that coherence is too readily embraced, however, it is important to recognize that these accents serve very different intentionalities and are not easily reconciled.

When we come to Christian extrapolation, the argument of Paul in Romans 4 and Galatians 3–4 is that the promise made to *Abraham* (the royal covenant of grace) is accepted as "the gospel beforehand," and the tradition of *Moses* is rejected (Gal 3:8).[23] It is clear that in Paul's time and circumstance this argument is concerned with contemporary Judaism and, indeed, it concerned competing claims within Judaism, one of which evolved into Christianity as it moved away from the synagogue. In Christian tradition and with particular reference to "The Tortured Conscience of the West," the tension of Mosaic Torah and Davidic promise is readily transposed into an interface of "law and gospel" in which "gospel" is everything.[24] The Calvinist tradition, in which this author stands, has wisely understood that the fundamental category of faith is *covenant*, under which the rubrics of *covenantal requirement* and free *covenantal promise* are to be sustained together.[25] In such an interpretation, the truth and reality of YHWH toward Israel is variously one of free gift and one of rigorous demand; no simplistic dominance of one or the other can finally be sustained. The relationship understood as covenant, not unlike every relationship that is based on exclusive commitment, is indeed an offer of free gift; but the free gift, characteristically, is in the context of exclusive loyalty that is enacted as obedience.

It is a great temptation to select from these traditions and their respective derivative trajectories in order to tilt the covenantal framing of worship in one direction or another, even though the completed covenantal tradition itself refuses such selectivity. Such selectivity is characteristically self-serving:

(a) If the Mosaic-Deuteronomic tradition of conditionality is taken by itself, the outcome is a demanding *quid pro quo* arrangement with no slippage for the mystery of the inscrutability between the two parties.[26]

(b) If the Abrahamic-Davidic tradition of unconditional promise is taken by itself, the outcome is a "blank check" that may issue in a kind of "cheap grace" where one finds one's self outside the Torah.[27]

Either of these options clearly distorts the thickness of this relationship, failing to understand on the one hand that true sovereignty cannot be mocked, failing on the other hand to understand that grace is costly to the giver who is drawn into pathos over the brokenness. There is no doubt that interpretive agility is required in order to bear witness and give practice to the richness of this relationship.

(c) One other temptation is readily discerible, given this interface of conditionality and unconditionality. It is to turn the unconditional tradition of promise toward one's self and to apply the conditional requirement of obedience to others. Or even more scandalously, in the sphere of politics and economics to which covenant also pertains, there is a temptation to take the tradition of unconditional promise as an affirmation of the "haves" who are entitled and to assign the tradition of conditional requirement to the "have-nots."[28] Such an interpretive arrangement may insist that the "have-nots" would "have," if only they were obedient, that is, not lazy.

It is clear that the completed tradition, with its complex intertwining of trajectories, requires rich, imaginative interpretation in order to let the tradition surface appropriately in a variety of contexts. One can see how this might be done in the parable of Luke 16:19-31.[29] In this parable, the Lucan tradition utilizes both voices of covenant. The *Abrahamic* (unconditional) tradition is related to the poor man; only the *Mosaic* (conditional) tradition is offered to the rich man. The parable demonstrates a remarkably agile hermeneutical management of the two traditions; such management of the tradition is crucial in order to maintain the "play" of this complexity of tradition, to let the truth of the tradition touch different folk in different contexts differently.

(5) *The play of presence and absence.* Israel's worship is conducted in confidence that YHWH is present in holy times and holy places for genuine communion, and for direct interaction in response to the prayers and praises of Israel. A great deal of energy is given over to Presence in the cultic traditions, most especially in the Priestly traditions of Exodus 25–31, 36–40. These texts feature the construction and completion of an adequate place that can be a habitat for the divine holiness. The Psalms, moreover, give evidence of Israel joyously entering the presence (Pss 95:1-2; 118:19; 122:1). The fullest articulation of divine presence is perhaps in 1 Kings 8:12-13, which celebrates that YHWH "dwells" in the Jerusalem Temple "forever and ever."

Nonetheless, one can detect an uneasiness in Israel's worship traditions in the Old Testament concerning the divine presence. This uneasiness is rooted on the one hand in the affirmation of YHWH's freedom who is the God who goes to and fro in the land (2 Sam 7:6-7), and who will not be "held" or domesticated by any cultic arrangement. This accent on the freedom of YHWH is a function of and reflection upon the conviction that there can be no "graven images" of YHWH.[30] On the other hand, the uneasiness about divine presence is rooted in raw, lived experience of absence, a reality reflected in the tradition of lament.

Because of uneasiness about divine presence due to YHWH's

73

freedom, the cultic traditions of Israel devised strategies and formulations that articulated YHWH's cultic presence-cum-freedom. Gerhard von Rad has seen that the Priestly tradition revolved around the coming of *divine glory*, while allowing that YHWH's own self was not committed to the holy place (Exod 40:34-38). Conversely, the Deuteronomic tradition focused upon the presence of the *divine name* that would be present to Israel while acknowledging YHWH's own self to be present elsewhere:[31]

> But will God indeed dwell on the earth? Even heaven and the highest heaven cannot contain you, much less this house that I have built! Regard your servant's prayer and his plea, O LORD my God, heeding the cry and the prayer that your servant prays to you today; that your eyes may be open night and day toward this house, the place of which you said, "My name shall be there," that you may heed the prayer that your servant prays toward this place. Hear the plea of your servant and of your people Israel when they pray toward this place; O hear in heaven your dwelling place; heed and forgive. (1 Kgs 8:27-30; see Deut 26:15)

Both of these strategies sought to affirm at the same time the genuine engagement of YHWH with Israel in worship and the freedom of YHWH not to be domesticated by any of the "mechanisms" of presence. The problem is an acute one, due to the character of YHWH who is at the same time committed to *covenantal mutuality* with Israel and yet who presides over Israel in a relationship of acute and *uncompromising incommensurability*.[32] This arrangement permitted all the confidence in worship that was necessary to boldness and assurance; at the same time it precluded any presumption on the part of Israel that it had penetrated the mystery of YHWH's own life.

The more acute form of absence, voiced in Israel's laments and in a more extreme form in the utterances of Job, is the undeniable absence of YHWH in the life of Israel and in the life of the world. This is a quotidian datum of lived reality—perhaps most acutely enacted in our time in the Jewish Shoah; it evidences that the world, and our lives in it are sometimes left in the void, without presence, without assurance, without buoyancy, and without possibility. Such lived reality cannot be denied or explained away by clever theological reasoning that can say only that it "seems" like God is absent.[33] Israel does not attest that YHWH "seems" to be absent! And of course, the wonder of the Old Testament is that Israel did not flinch from the shrill verbal acknowledgment of divine absence. Israel issued a protest against such absence (or silence), because Israel knew itself to be entitled to YHWH's presence.[34] Thus Job can pray for presence:

> Only grant two things to me,
>   then I will not hide myself from your face:
> withdraw your hand far from me,
>   and do not let dread of you terrify me.
> Then call, and I will answer;
>   or let me speak, and you reply to me. (Job 13:20-22)

Job can yearn for access to divine presence (Job 31:35-37). But of course when Job finally secures a response to his demand, it is a divine response that concedes nothing to his need or expectation (Job 38–41). In Israel's startling candor, the Old Testament stands as a protest against absence, but also as a protest against any "easy" presence.

The matter is most acute in Israel's exile. On the one hand, Ezekiel, in the Priestly tradition, can attest that the glory of YHWH departs from the Jerusalem Temple and from Israel's presence because the defiled city can no longer be an acceptable residence for the holy God (Ezek 9–10). On the other hand, the tradition of Isaiah, taking up the prophetic imagery of marriage, can attest that YHWH is a husband who has abandoned his "wife," in this text without any accusation against Israel that would justify abandonment:

> For a brief moment I abandoned you,
>> but with great compassion I will gather you.
> In overflowing wrath for a moment
>> I hid my face from you,
> but with everlasting love I will have compassion on you,
>> says the LORD, your Redeemer. (Isa 54:7-8)

To be sure, Ezekiel has also seen that divine holiness returns to the Temple (Ezek 43-44). The Isaiah tradition, moreover, attests that the divine abandonment of Israel was only "for a moment" (Isa 54:7-8). Nonetheless Israel was left to wonder how it was to be "without God in the world."

This tension of *presence and absence* was an acute one for the ongoing traditions of worship in the church.[35] In the contemporary world there are of course endless attempts to capture the divine presence for any particular "absolute" we may fancy. In the church, such ploys of absolutism may include those of dogma, morality, liturgical practice, or spirituality. Beyond the particularities of the church, such "ideologies of presence" can imagine that God inhabits nationalism or capitalism or a myriad of other "isms," each of which seems to its proponents to be invested with divine force and authority. Israel knows that the capacity to articulate, signify, and experience divine presence is problematic and must not be presumed upon. It is no surprise that Samuel Terrien, in his exquisite study, must finally characterize the divine presence as "elusive."[36]

The Old Testament knows that direct divine presence is rare; it is offered only occasionally to Israel or to individual persons in the overwhelmingness of theophany. More characteristically, YHWH's presence is known to Israel in its several worship traditions only through signs, not immediately but *mediated* through visible signs of invisible presence. It is for that reason that the church has struggled with the meaning of the Eucharist; the Eucharist was occasion for acute polemics in the sixteenth century, and the church still entertains a range of alternative understandings of the bread and wine, all the way from a materialistic transubstantiation to a Zwinglian notion of memorial. On any reading, the sign of

Eucharist is attestation of God's presence in the *ordinariness* of lived reality in bread and wine. In that assured presence, however, the church dare not be presumptuous about divine presence. For good reason, the meal characteristically begins with, "We do not presume to come to this table...." At its best, the church takes care not "to eat and drink unworthily" (1 Cor 11:27-29). It is urgent to maintain this "play" of tension in worship. When the freedom of God is collapsed into institutional management, the host institution of the church is readily seduced into an absolutism in which "infallibility" takes many forms. At the same time it is clear that absence per se leaves the world profane and with a possible future. Thus the "play" of worship must leave us always amid the Elusive. If the play is collapsed in explanatory, managing modes, the elusive reality becomes an illusion.

(6) *The play of praise and lament.* I have already suggested that praise and lament are two characteristic modes of Israel's speech in worship. I return to that pair of rhetorical practices now in light of the comments above concerning *presence and absence.* The praise of Israel, the glad, exuberant ceding of life over to YHWH, sings of YHWH's actions and YHWH's wondrous character. These praises, surely sounded in Temple worship, are addressed to YHWH. In addressing YHWH, Israel affirms YHWH's presence with Israel.

Conversely, the laments of Israel, perhaps sounded in Temple worship or perhaps in a "lesser" mode of worship (such as family or clan), are petitions addressed to YHWH in time of trouble. These prayers are indeed addressed to YHWH and so assume something of YHWH's presence. They voice trouble that is possible only because of YHWH's neglect, silence, or absence. Thus they are appeals that the God who is neglectful should be attentive, that the God who is silent should speak, that the God who is absent should become present in full power.[37]

As the double theme of "presence and absence" attests not only to the candor of Israel in worship but also to the elusiveness of YHWH, so "praise and lament" attest to the wonder and problematic of life with YHWH. There are, to be sure, complete

77

hymns of praise and quite complete lament prayers. Our attention here, however, concerns Israel's capacity to speak, in noticeably disjunctive fashion, praise and lament in the same utterance; such utterance is at the same time a *celebration of* YHWH's *decisive presence* with Israel and an *acknowledgment of* YHWH's *silence-cum-absence*. As concerns Israel, such utterance is both an act of glad *ceding* of life to YHWH and a determined *claiming* of life for Israel and for self.[38] The *celebration* and the *acknowledgment*, the *ceding* and the *claiming*, constitute no con- tradiction in the relationship; together they exhibit the play that perforce inescapably belongs to a serious, exclusive relation- ship marked by both freedom and commitment.

Westermann has shown how the full pattern of lament psalm moves characteristically from plea to praise, from claiming to ceding, from acknowledgment to celebration.[39] This is evident, for example, in Psalm 13:

> [Lament]:
> How long, O LORD? Will you forget me forever?
>> How long will you hide your face from me?
> How long must I bear pain in my soul,
>> and have sorrow in my heart all day long?
> How long shall my enemy be exalted over me?
> Consider and answer me, O LORD my God!
>> Give light to my eyes, or I will sleep the sleep of death,
> and my enemy will say, "I have prevailed";
>> my foes will rejoice because I am shaken. (Ps 13:1-4)
> [Praise]:
> But I trusted in your steadfast love;
>> my heart shall rejoice in your salvation.
> I will sing to the LORD,
>> because he has dealt bountifully with me. (Ps 13:5-6)

The same move is more fully voiced in Psalm 22 in which the complaint extends through verse 21*a*, and then turns abruptly to praise in verse 21*b*. Patrick Miller has seen that in verse 1 the psalmist voices YHWH's abandonment, but the Psalm is nevertheless addressed to "my God," counting fully upon the relationship that endures in the midst of abandonment.[40] While the reverse movement occurs less frequently, the movement of the psalm can also be from praise (or thanks) to plea. A clear example is in Psalm 40. Verses 1-10 gladly acknowledge YHWH's deliverances:

> I have told the glad news of deliverance
>   in the great congregation;
> see, I have not restrained my lips,
>   as you know, O LORD.
> I have not hidden your saving
>   help within my heart,
> I have spoken of your faithfulness and your salvation;
> I have not concealed your steadfast love and your faithfulness
>   from the great congregation. (Ps 40:9-10)

But then, in verse 11, the voice of Israel turns to petition that is reinforced by the lament of verse 12. The petition of verse 10 is taken up again in verse 13: "Be pleased, O LORD, to deliver me; O LORD, make haste to help me" (Ps 40:13).

The Psalms, Israel's characteristic utterance in worship, are the voice of extremity in Israel. Worship of YHWH, moreover, is engagement in the relational extremities of life in which there are two parties engaged with intensity and candor. For that reason, it is appropriate that Israel, in its liturgic utterances, should rebound from one extremity to the other. Such rhetoric of course violates our sense of order, reason, propriety, and symmetry. The immediacy of intense personal rhetoric, however, will not be restrained from such hyperbole. In a technological environment of interpretation that wants to reduce speech to sound byte and thin communication, this capacity for vigorous verbal interaction invites the community of worship into the full range of its life toward the God who governs all. Such liturgic speech constitutes a model for an alternative way in which to utter and therefore to live reality.[41]

It is perhaps of special importance to notice that the great

79

propensity in the church, in its practice, is to preclude the shrill disjunctive speech of worship by reducing lament to confession and to slot trouble always as guilt. Such a liturgical maneuver places a powerful restraint upon the honesty of Israel's speech to YHWH "from whom no secret can be hid." In its sense of covenantal entitlement, Israel refused to reduce its trouble to its own failure. It understood that more complexity than simple acknowledgment of failure must be recognized amid trouble; that complexity, moreover, includes reference to the "enemies" of YHWH and of Israel, and the daring thought much on the minds of Israel, that YHWH is not, in every case, fully reliable. Such awareness surely belongs to covenantal candor. It is clear that Israel did not cringe in its truth-telling, because it knew that it had entitlements in that relationship. Such entitlements, however, did not prevent these same speeches and prayers from turning to extravagant praise by those glad to be the people of YHWH. This interaction cut deeply below politeness and symmetry to the reality of trust and commitment. The nimbleness of this "play" of praise and lament belongs to the fullness of the covenantal transaction that marks the life of both parties who are engaged in worship interaction together.

(7) *The play of memory and hope.* Israel's worship is an act of deep, intentional remembering. The utterance of credo that eventuates in the great psalms of remembering evidences that Israel is rooted in the blessings of creation and in the deliverances of history (Pss 78, 105, 106, 136).[42] These remembrances are kept available with contemporary generative power in the worship of Israel. Israel's intense remembering is no exercise in either escape into the past or retreat from the present and future. Rather, Israel's remembering is clearly grounded in the conviction that what has been attested from the past is the clue to the future. What has been given Israel in the past is what will be given in the future; what YHWH has done in the past is what YHWH will do in the future.

The clearest case of this dialectic of past and future is in

Lamentations 3:18-24, a prayer uttered in the sixth century BCE in the midst of the destroyed Temple and city. The speaker, surely personified Israel, is bereft of all hope: "So I say, 'Gone is my glory, and all that I had hoped for from the LORD'" (Lam 3:18).[43] In the midst of the despair, however, the speaker "calls to mind" the great wonders of YHWH's life with Israel:

> But this I call to mind,
> > and therefore I have hope:
> The steadfast love of the LORD never ceases,
> > his mercies never come to an end;
> they are new every morning;
> > great is your faithfulness. (Lam 3:21-23)

The memory now recalled is expressed in the shorthand of "steadfast love, mercies, faithfulness"; that shorthand arises as a summary of much more specific recitals of the past. This shorthand summary, in turn, produces buoyancy for the immediate future: "'The LORD is my portion,' says my soul, 'therefore I will hope in him'" (Lam 3:24).

This triad of terms alludes to all of the great wonders of YHWH toward Israel that elsewhere are given in more detail, deeds and gifts of YHWH that are taken as measures of YHWH's steadfast love.[44]

This remembering is the ground of hope that persists in every circumstance of despair. The despair can be real:

> As a deer longs for flowing streams,
> > so my soul longs for you, O God.
> My soul thirsts for God,
> > for the living God.
> When shall I come and behold the face of God?
> My tears have been my food
> > day and night,
> while people say to me continually,
> > "Where is your God?" (Ps 42:1-3)

81

Even in such a context, however, YHWH is remembered as help, and so is the ground of hope:

> Why are you cast down, O my soul,
>> and why are you disquieted within me?
> Hope in God; for I shall again praise him,
>> my help and my God. (Ps 42:5; see Pss 42:11*b*; 43:5*b*)

The reason that this relationship of past and present is crucial is that the worshiping community always faces three temptations concerning its time with YHWH:

(a) The community may suffer from *amnesia* and so disregard its past and become rootless and autonomous. The tradition of Deuteronomy understood very well that affluence produces amnesia that in turn invites a sense of autonomy:

> You shall eat your fill and bless the LORD your God for the good land that he has given you.... Do not say to yourself, "My power and the might of my own hand have gotten me this wealth." (Deut 8:10, 17)

(b) The community may retreat into the past that becomes a frozen act of *nostalgia*, unable to imagine a future from YHWH that will be different from the past, seeking only a return to how it was in the past:

> If I forget you, O Jerusalem,
>> let my right hand wither!
> Let my tongue cling to the roof of my mouth,
>> if I do not remember you,
> if I do not set Jerusalem
>> above my highest joy. (Ps 137:5-6)

(c) The community may collapse a forgotten past and an unhoped future into a *timeless present tense*, either a timeless present of despair or of self-congratulations:

All streams run to the sea,
  but the sea is not full;
to the place where the streams flow,
  there they continue to flow.
All things are wearisome;
  more than one can express;
the eye is not satisfied with seeing,
  or the ear filled with hearing.
What has been is what will be,
  and what has been done is what will be done;
  there is nothing new under the sun.
Is there a thing of which it is said,
  "See, this is new"?
It has already been,
  in the ages before us.
The people of long ago are not remembered,
  nor will there be any remembrance
of people yet to come
  by those who come after them. (Eccl 1:7-11)

The recited memory of Israel as ground for hope is a form of resistance against these three temptations. Sandwiched between a vibrant memory and a buoyant hope in YHWH, moreover, the present tense in Israel's life is characterized as a freighted opportunity for trust, joy, and obedience. We may perhaps take the characterization of Jesus in the Fourth Gospel as an epitome of Israel's sense of rootedness and destiny: "Jesus, knowing that the Father had given all things into his hands, and that he had come from God and was going to God, got up from the table, took off his outer robe, and tied a towel around himself" (John 13:3-4).

Long before this dramatic episode of footwashing, Israel had long known it had "come from God" and knew it was "going to God." Consequently, Israel was situated for obedience in the present. The dramatic play of past and future keeps Israel from escaping into nostalgia, from fleeing to a paradisiacal future, and from reneging on the present. There are, in this liturgical practice, distinct seasons, all connected and referring to each other, each in its own way distinct and to be savored for itself.

The worship of Israel is thick; it resists every reductionism, even those that become conventional in the church. The practice of thickness is inescapable because of the character of God in all of God's holiness; as a result, interaction with Yhwh is necessarily always given in signs. The principle sign in this worship tradition, surrounded by many other signs, is a meal. It is a meal that, as we have seen, stretches all the way from ancient *tôdah* to the church's Eucharist.[45] The meal of thanks brings the depth of faith to the concreteness of daily bread. The truth of daily bread is that it is indispensable to our life and is only given by this God:

> The eyes of all look to you,
>> and you give them their food in due season.
> You open your hand,
>> satisfying the desire of every living thing. (Ps 145:15-16)

The bread, so necessary and so thick, requires utterance. The church nonetheless has always known that its utterance is finally inadequate to the bread. The church confesses that he was "known to us in the breaking of bread," but it does not know *how* known, just known (Luke 24:35). Thus the most elemental sign of covenant is thick and elusive. The capacity to receive and host this particular thickness and this particular elusiveness generates a quite particular community, one not given to the thinness of any cultural environment. The sum of this thickness and elusiveness has been caught in a parabolic narrative way by Isak Denison, of course in a parable when the village was at table.[46] It is no wonder that the returning visitor in Denison's tale, *Babette's Feast*, could do no better than to quote the psalter:

> Steadfast love and faithfulness will meet;
>> righteousness and peace will kiss each other.
> Faithfulness will spring up from the ground,
>> and righteousness will look down from the sky. (Ps 85:10-11)

The worship of Israel is, at the same time, in such common gifts of the table, an act of defiance of every failed world and an act of entering an alternative world. The church, similarly, is set in bread and wine as a sign among us of steadfast love, faithfulness, righteousness, and peace. These are the staples that sustain our life and for which we render glad, obedient thanks. It is no wonder that in this thick world of signs, a community of faith is summoned to "lift up your hearts!" It is no wonder either that in response to the summons the community gladly, willingly, and obediently answers, "We lift them up unto the Lord."

Notes

Acknowledgments

1. Patrick D. Miller, *The Religion of Ancient Israel* (Louisville: Westminster John Knox, 2000).
2. Patrick D. Miller, *They Cried to the Lord: The Form and Theology of Biblical Prayer* (Minneapolis: Fortress Press, 1994).

1. Orthodox Yahwism in Dialogic Modes

1. See Samuel Terrien, *The Elusive Presence: Toward a New Biblical Theology* (New York: Harper & Row, 1978).
2. The most important critical literature includes the following: Rainer Albertz, *A History of Israelite Religion in the Old Testament Period I: From the Beginnings to the End of the Monarchy* (Louisville: Westminster John Knox Press, 1994); idem., *A History of Israelite Religion in the Old Testament Period II: From the Exile to the Maccabees* (Louisville: Westminster John Knox Press, 1994); Erhard Gerstenberger, *Theologies of the Old Testament* (Minneapolis: Fortress Press, 2002); Walter Harrelson, *From Fertility Cult to Worship* (Garden City: Doubleday, 1969); Hans-Joachim Kraus, *Worship in Israel: A Cultic History of the Old Testament* (Oxford: Blackwell, 1966); Patrick D. Miller, *The Religion of Ancient Israel* (Library of Ancient Israel; Louisville: Westminster John Knox Press, 2000); H. H. Rowley, *Worship in Ancient Israel: Its Forms and Meaning* (London: SPCK, 1967); and Roland de Vaux, *Ancient Israel: Its Life and Institutions* (London: Darton, Longman, and Todd, 1961).
3. Of the works listed above, only those of Gerstenberger and Harrelson make any substantial move toward what might be

regarded as normative in the worship of ancient Israel. See also James Muilenburg, *The Way of Israel: Biblical Faith and Ethics* (London: Routledge & Kegan Paul, 1962).

4. That classic hypothesis was decisively articulated by Julius Wellhausen, *Prolegomena to the History of Israel* (Durham: Duke University Press, 1994). The hypothesis has been summarized in a most accessible and helpful way by John H. Hayes, *An Introduction to Old Testament Study* (Nashville: Abingdon Press, 1979), 159-80.

5. This is especially noteworthy in the discussions of Albertz and Gerstenberger cited above.

6. Gerstenberger, *Theologies of the Old Testament,* proposes a complete taxonomy of such subcommunities in Israel.

7. Harrelson, *From Fertility Cult to Worship*, xiii.

8. See Hans Georg Gadamer, *The Relevance of the Beautiful and Other Essays* (Cambridge: Cambridge University Press, 1986); Peter L. Berger, *A Rumor of Angels: Modern Society and the Rediscovery of the Supernatural* (New York: Pelican Books, 1971).

9. This is evident in the well-known, great mythic texts from Mesopotamia of which the best known is the *Enuma Elish.* These mythic statements surely functioned liturgically for the founding and legitimating of divine order and, in a derivative way, political, social order as well.

10. It is plausible that these generally shared myths functioned in Israel's tradition even before the monarchy; thus for example, Frank M. Cross, *From Canaanite Myth to Hebrew Epic* (Cambridge: Harvard University Press, 1973), 121-44, can speak of the repeated "recrudescence" of "the myth of the sea." Nonetheless, it is clear that it was with the rise of the monarchy that these cosmic myths began to play a central part in temple worship and with the divine legitimization of the Jerusalem establishment.

11. On the Ras Shamra texts and their significance for the religious milieu of emerging Israel, see D. Pardee and Pierre Bordreuil, "Ugarit, Texts and Literature," in vol. 6, pp. 706-21 of the *Anchor Bible Dictionary*, ed. David Noel Freedman (New York: Doubleday, 1992), and the works cited there; and N. Wyatt et al., eds., *Ugarit, Religion and Culture: Proceedings of the International Colloquium on Ugarit, Religion and Culture,* Edinburgh, July, 1994 (Munster: Ugarit-Verlag, 1996).

12. See as representative of this approach, Norman Habel, *Yahweh Versus Baal: A Study of the Relevance of Ugaritic Materials for the Early Faith of Israel* (New York: Bookman Associates, 1964); and more programmatically, see G. Ernest Wright, *The Old Testament Against Its Environment* (Studies in Biblical Theology 2; London: SCM Press, 1950).

13. For example, see the classic study of Rene Daussaud, *Les origines Cananeenes du sacrifice Israelite* (Paris: Ernest Leroux, 1921).

14. The habit in Old Testament study of making a sharp contrast between "Canaanite Religion" and "the Faith of Israel" was surely given important impetus by the polemic of Karl Barth against "religion." It is likely that the contrast made by Gerhard von Rad between the credo recital of early Israel and the Canaanite environment of that faith is reflective of the struggle in the 1930s with German Socialism, a struggle much shaped by Barth and certainly reflected in the early work of von Rad. See Walter Brueggemann, "The Loss and Recovery of Creation in Old Testament Theology," *Theology Today* 53 (1996): 177-90.

15. See the general argument of Harrelson, *From Fertility Cult to Worship*, and more specifically, the analysis of Patrick D. Miller, *The Religion of Ancient Israel*, 48-51.

16. Ibid., 48-51.

17. Ibid, 48.

18. Ibid.

19. Ibid.

20. Ibid., 50.

21. Ibid.

22. Ibid., 50-51.

23. On the aniconic accent in Yahwism from the outset, see Patrick D. Miller, "Israelite Religion," *The Hebrew Bible and Its Modern Interpreters*, ed. Douglas A. Knight and Gene M. Tucker (Philadelphia: Fortress Press, 1985), 211-13.

24. On recent scholarly judgment on monotheism in Israel, see Bernhard Lang (ed.), *Einzige Gott: die Geburt des biblische Monotheismus* (Munich: Koesel, 1981); idem., *Monotheism and the Prophetic Minority: An Essay in Biblical History and Sociology* (Sheffield: Almond Press, 1983); Mark S. Smith, *The Origins of Biblical Monotheism: Israel's Polytheistic Background and the*

Ugaritic Texts (Cambridge: Cambridge University Press, 2000); idem., *Early History of God: Yahweh and the Other Deities in Ancient Israel* (San Francisco: Harper & Row, 1990).

25. Roland de Vaux, *Ancient Israel: Its Life and Institutions*, 271, articulates the primal claims of Israel's faith somewhat differently from that of Miller, but is agreed on the main points: Israel worshiped a God who was the only God; this God intervened in history as the God of the covenant; this God and the worship of this God permit no images.

26. Rowley, *Worship in Ancient Israel*, 251.

27. The classic text is Exodus 34:6-7, on which see Walter Brueggemann, *Theology of the Old Testament: Testimony, Dispute, Advocacy* (Minneapolis: Fortress Press, 1997), 213-28.

28. On "covenant," see Delbert R. Hillers, *Covenant: The History of a Biblical Idea* (Baltimore: Johns Hopkins University Press, 1969); Ernest W. Nicholson, *God and His People: Covenant and Theology in the Old Testament* (Oxford: Clarendon Press, 1986); Rolf Rendtorff, *The Covenant Formula: An Exegetical and Theological Investigation* (Edinburgh: T. & T. Clark, 1998); and Steven L. McKenzie, *Covenant* (St. Louis: Chalice Press, 2000).

29. See Roland de Vaux, *Ancient Israel: Its Life and Institutions*, 272.

30. Patrick Miller, *The Religion of Ancient Israel*, 5.

31. At mid-twentieth century, it was a widespread notion among scholars that Israel practiced a regular ceremony of covenantal renewal. See Hans-Joachim Kraus, *Worship in Israel: A Cultic History of the Old Testament* (Oxford: Blackwell, 1966), 208-22; idem., *Die Koenigsherrschaft Gottes im Alten Testament: Untersuchen zu der Liedern von Jahwes Thronbesteigung* (Tubingen: J.C.B. Mohr, 1951); and John Gray, *The Biblical Doctrine of the Reign of God* (Edinburgh: T. & T. Clark, 1979). While scholarly ardor for such a hypothesis has cooled, it is nonetheless plausible to think that liturgic reenactment in some form must have been constant in Israel.

32. On these metaphors for YHWH, see Walter Brueggemann, *Theology of the Old Testament*, 233-50; G. Ernest Wright, *The Old Testament and Theology* (New York: Harper & Row, 1969), 70-150; and Patrick D. Miller, "The Sovereignty of God," *The Hermeneutical Quest: Essays in Honor of James Luther Mays*, ed. by Donald G. Miller (Allison Park: Pickwick Publications, 1986), 129-44.

33. See Brueggemann, *Theology of the Old Testament*, 250-61; and Robert Banks, *God the Worker: Journeys into the Mind, Heart, and Imagination of God* (Valley Forge: Judson Press, 1994).
34. Harrelson, *From Fertility Cult to Worship*, 114-15.

2. The Gestures of Worship and Sacrifice

1. The historicizing is most pronounced with the festival of Passover, whereby the utterances of Israel closely ties the festival to the recital of the Exodus memory.
2. Clearly, the historicizing that accented historical deliverances did not eliminate from the horizon of Israel the blessings of creation. An older generation of scholars under the impetus of Karl Barth moved completely away from creation themes, but see Claus Westermann, "Creation and History in the Old Testament," *The Gospel and Human Destiny*, ed. by Vilmos Vajta (Minneapolis: Augsburg Publishing House, 1971), 11-38, for an early programmatic statement of the twinning of these themes in the life and faith of Israel.
3. I am not listing Sabbath as a distinct festival, because it seems likely that Sabbath concerned work stoppage more than worship in early Israel. In any case, the worship of Israel is shot through with "the sabbatic principle."
4. On this theme and with particular reference to Isaiah 58, see Kathleen O'Connor, ed., *Breaking Bread, Building Justice: Mission of the Church in a World of Hungers* (unpublished papers).
5. On the multidimensional reality of holiness in the Old Testament, see John G. Gammie, *Holiness in Israel* (Overtures to Biblical Theology; Minneapolis: Fortress Press, 1981).
6. On these two dominant interpretive trajectories, see Norbert Lohfink, *Theology of the Pentateuch: Themes of the Priestly Narrative and Deuteronomy* (Minneapolis: Fortress Press, 1994).
7. See Jeffries M. Hamilton, *Social Justice and Deuteronomy: The Case of Deuteronomy 15* (SBL Dissertation Series 136; Atlanta: Scholars Press, 1992).
8. Roland de Vaux, *Ancient Israel: Its Life and Institutions*, 451; on the larger social significance of gift, see Marcel Mauss, *The Gift: Forms and Functions of Exchange in Archaic Societies* (London: Cohen and West, 1966).

9. The addendum of verses 18-19 clearly assumes the restored, rebuilt temple.

3. The Utterance of Yhwh in Worship

1. On utterance and gesture, word and sacrament, see Paul Ricoeur, "Manifestation and Proclamation," *Figuring the Sacred: Religion, Narrative, and Imagination* (Minneapolis: Fortress Press, 1995), 48-67. Or in another mode, see Samuel Terrien, *The Elusive Presence*, on "religion of the ear" and "religion of the eye."

2. Such mediation is done through priestly orders, some of which overlap and some of which compete with each other. The characterization of the priesthood in the Old Testament is enormously complex. One dominant hypothesis concerning that priesthood is that of Frank Moore Cross, *From Canaanite Myth to Hebrew Epic* (Cambridge: Harvard University Press, 1973), 195-215. See also Richard D. Nelson, *Raising Up a Faithful Priest: Community and Priesthood in Biblical Theology* (Louisville: Westminster John Knox Press, 1993), and William R. Millar, *Priesthood in Ancient Israel* (St. Louis: Chalice Press, 2001).

3. See Frank Crüsemann, *The Torah: Theology and Social History of Old Testament Law* (Edinburgh: T. & T. Clark, 1996), 351-57.

4. Also pertinent is Psalm 81; on the hypothesis of a festival of covenant renewal, see the summary statement of Kraus, *Die Koenigsherrschaft Gottes im Alten Testament*.

5. See Crüsemann, *The Torah: Theology and Social History of Old Testament Law*.

6. See Patrick D. Miller, *The Religion of Ancient Israel*, 168-69.

7. See Crüsemann, *The Torah: Theology and Social History of Old Testament Law*, 277-327.

8. Ibid., 201-75.

9. Gerhard von Rad, *Studies in Deuteronomy* (Studies in Biblical Theology 9; Chicago: Henry Regnery Company, 1953), 16.

10. While the priestly office is clearly charged with such oracles, it is also clear that the priests had monopoly on such oracles; the prophets also delivered such oracles. Whether they did so in the context of worship is a disputed point.

11. See Aubrey R. Johnson, *The Cultic Prophet in Ancient Israel*

(Cardiff: University of Wales Press, 1962), for a proposal of cultic contexts for prophets.

12. See Patrick D. Miller, *They Cried to the Lord: The Form and Theology of Biblical Prayer* (Minneapolis: Fortress Press, 1994), chapter 4.

13. Ibid., 86-114.

14. Fredrik Lindström, *Suffering and Sin: Interpretations of Illness in the Individual Complaint Psalms* (Coniectanea Biblica, Old Testament Series 37; Stockholm: Almqvist & Wiksell, 1994), 435-39 and *passim*, notes the cruciality of the Temple for salvation in the Psalter.

15. Gerstenberger, *Theologies of the Old Testament*, 207-72.

16. Miller, *They Cried to the Lord*, 228-32.

4. The Utterance of Israel in Worship

1. Gerhard von Rad, "The Form-Critical Problem of the Hexateuch," *The Form-Critical Problem of the Hexateuch and Other Essays* (New York: McGraw-Hill, 1966), 1-78.

2. Ibid.

3. It is crucial for appreciating von Rad's great work on confession to remember that his hypothesis of "credo" in ancient Israel was in the immediate context of the confessing movement of the German Church in the face of National Socialism, and that with particular reference to the Barmen Declaration.

4. The affirmation of the blessings of creation has been especially voiced by Walter Harrelson, *From Fertility Religion to Worship*; and Claus Westermann, *Blessing in the Bible and the Life of the Church* (Overtures to Biblical Theology; Philadelphia: Fortress Press, 1978).

5. Michael Fishbane, *Text and Texture: Close Readings of Selected Biblical Text* (New York: Schocken Books, 1978), 79-83, has proposed that instruction to children in Deuteronomy 6:4-5, for example, indicates that the children were resistant and did not want such identification with the faith of the adult community. He refers to such children as "*distemporaries.*" The text wants to transform them to "*contemporaries.*"

6. On the dynamism of this chapter, see Walter Brueggemann, *Biblical Perspectives on Evangelism: Living in a Three-Storied Universe* (Nashville: Abingdon Press, 1993), 48-70.

7. Claus Westermann, *The Psalms: Structure, Context and Message* (Minneapolis: Augsburg Publishing House, 1980), 73-83.
8. See Patrick D. Miller, *They Cried to the Lord: The Form and Theology of Biblical Prayer* (Minneapolis: Fortress Press), 188.
9. See Walter Brueggemann, "Praise and the Psalms: A Politics of Glad Abandonment," *The Psalms & the Life of Faith*, ed. by Patrick D. Miller (Minneapolis: Fortress Press, 1995), 112-32.
10. On the summons to praise, see Walter Brueggemann, *Israel's Praise: Doxology Against Idolatry and Ideology* (Philadelphia: Fortress Press, 1989), 78-87.
11. Ibid., 90-100.
12. See Peter L. Berger and Thomas Luckmann, *The Social Construction of Reality: A Treatise in the Sociology of Knowledge* (Garden City: Doubleday, 1966), and Amos N. Wilder, "Story and Story-World," *Interpretation* 37 (1983): 353-64.
13. See Walter Wink, *Naming the Powers: The Language of Power in the New Testament* (Philadelphia: Fortress Press, 1984); idem., *Unmasking the Powers: The Invisible Forces that Determine Human Existence* (Philadelphia: Fortress Press, 1986); idem., *Engaging the Powers: Dissent and Resistance in a World of Domination* (Minneapolis: Fortress Press, 1992).
14. Claus Westermann, "The Role of Lament in the Theology of the Old Testament," *Interpretation* 28 (1974): 33, comments:

> The result is that both in Christian dogmatics and in Christian worship suffering as opposed to sin has receded far into the background. The impression thus given is that ... the crucified and resurrected Lord ... was concerned with sin and not at all with suffering.

15. Fredrik Lindström, *Suffering and Sin: Interpretations of Illness in the Individual Complaint Psalms,* has demonstrated that Israel's complaints about trouble do not characteristically connect trouble to sin and guilt. The trouble is more often understood as unmerited, caused either by the aggression of "the enemy" or by the neglect of YHWH.
16. See Krister Stendahl, "Paul and the Introspective Conscience of the West," *Paul Among Jews and Gentiles and Other Essays* (Philadelphia: Fortress Press, 1976), 78-96.
17. Kathleen O'Connor, *Lamentations & The Tears of the World* (New

York: Orbis, 2002). See also Tod Linafelt, *Surviving Lamentations: Catastrophe, Lament, and Protest in the Afterlife of a Biblical Book* (Chicago: University of Chicago Press, 2000).

18. The identification of the enemy is open to imaginative interpretation, and may variously refer to an historical or a mythological threat, one from inside the community or an external adversary.

19. See Erich Zenger, *A God of Vengeance: Understanding the Psalms of Divine Wrath* (Louisville: Westminster John Knox Press, 1996).

20. See Walter Brueggemann, *Praying the Psalms* (Winona, Minnesota: Saint Mary's Press, 1993), 67-80.

21. Claus Westermann, "The Role of Lament in the Theology of the Old Testament," 34, concludes: "We have to decide anew whether the onesidedness of relating the work of Christ alone to the exclusion of any relation to man's suffering actually represents the New Testament as a whole and, if so, whether that understanding would not have to be corrected by the Old Testament. A correction of this sort would have far-reaching consequences."

22. For a study of such speech in social emergency, see Nancy Lee, *The Singers of Lamentations: Cities Under Siege, From Ur to Jerusalem to Sarajevo* (Biblical Interpretation Series 60; Leiden: Brill, 2002).

23. See Patrick D. Miller, *They Cried to the Lord*, 70-79.

24. On divine silence, see Andre Neher, *The Exile of the Word: From the Silence of the Bible to the Silence of Auschwitz* (Philadelphia: Jewish Publication Society of America, 1981), 24.

25. See the discussion of David Blumenthal, *Facing the Abusive God: A Theology of Protest* (Louisville: Westminster John Knox Press, 1993).

26. The phrase "second naiveté" is from Paul Ricoeur. See the review of the concept by Mark I. Wallace, *The Second Naiveté: Barth, Ricoeur, and the New Yale Theology* (Studies in American Biblical Hermeneutics 6; Macon: Mercer University Press, 1990).

27. Karl Barth, *Prayer* (50th Anniversary Edition; Louisville: Westminster John Knox Press, 2002), has demonstrated that petition is the most characteristic accent of evangelical prayer.

28. See Patrick D. Miller, *They Cried to the Lord*, 136-40.
29. Ibid., 99-114.
30. James Muilenburg, *The Way of Israel*, 107.
31. Claus Westermann, "Die Geschichtsbezogenheit menschlicher Reden von Gott im Alten Testament," *Weltgesprach* 1 (1967): 21, quoted by Hans Joachim Kraus, *Psalms 1-59: A Commentary* (Minneapolis: Augsburg Publishing House, 1988), 299.
32. Gerhard von Rad, "The Form-Critical Problem of the Hexateuch," 3-8.
33. Claus Westermann, *Praise and Lament in the Psalms* (Edinburgh: T. & T. Clark, 1981), 27-28.
34. Patrick D. Miller, *They Cried to the Lord*, 402-4, n. 2.
35. Harvey H. Guthrie, Jr., *Theology as Thanksgiving: From Israel's Psalms to the Church's Eucharist* (New York: Seabury Press, 1981).
36. Harmut Gese, "Psalm 22 und das Neue Testament," *Zeitschrift für Theologie und Kirche* 65 (1968): 1ff., quoted by Hans Joachim Kraus, *Psalms 1-59: A Commentary*, 301.
37. Harvey Guthrie, *Theology as Thanksgiving*, 14-24.
38. "Now Thank We All Our God," Martin Rinkart, 1636; trans. by Catherine Winkworth, 1858.
39. *The Book of Common Prayer* (New York: Seabury Press, 1979), 339.
40. Muilenburg, *The Way of Israel*, 126-27.

5. Worship: Israel at "Play"

1. David M. Gunn, *The Story of King David: Genre and Interpretation* (JSOT Supp. 6; Sheffield: University of Sheffield, 1978), 37-38, has shown how the biblical narrative is "entertainment" of a most serious kind.
2. See also Brent Strawn and Brad D. Strawn, "Preaching As Play: Winnecott, Scripture, and Homiletical Theory" (unpublished paper).
3. The prohibition of graven images is a somewhat enigmatic commandment. Among other things, it clearly is designed to protect and assert divine freedom.
4. See the comment of James Muilenburg at the end of chapter 4 concerning human freedom in the presence of God.
5. See above, p. 28.
6. See above, pp. 46-53.

7. See Dorothea Soelle, *Creative Disobedience* (Cleveland: Pilgrim Press, 1995).

8. On the Priestly horizon of holiness, see John G. Gammie, *Holiness in Israel* (Overtures to Biblical Theology; Minneapolis: Fortress Press, 1989), 9-44.

9. Concerning "graded holiness," see Philip P. Jenson, *Graded Holiness: A Key to the Priestly Conception of the World* (JSOT Supplement Series 106; Sheffield: Sheffield Academic Press, 1992), and Walter Houston, *Purity and Monotheism: Clean and Unclean Animals in Biblical Law* (JSOT Supplement Series 140; Sheffield: Sheffield Academic Press, 1993).

10. Norbert Lohfink, "Opfer und Saekularisierung im Deuteronomium," *Studien zu Opfer und Kult im Alten Testament*, ed. by Adrian Schenker (Tubingen: J. C. B. Mohr, 1992), 15-43.

11. See Walter Brueggemann, "Justice: The Earthly Form of God's Holiness," *The Covenanted Self: Explorations in Law and Covenant* (Minneapolis: Fortress Press, 1999), 48-58.

12. Mary Douglas, "Justice as the Cornerstone: An Interpretation of Leviticus 18-20," *Interpretation* 53 (1999), 341-50.

13. On the Jubilee, see Moshe Weinfeld, *Social Justice in Ancient Israel and in the Ancient Near East* (Minneapolis: Fortress Press, 1995).

14. Rainer Albertz, *A History of Israelite Religion in the Old Testament Period* (vols. 1 and 2; Louisville: Westminster John Knox Press, 1994); Erhard Gerstenberger, *Theologies of the Old Testament* (Minneapolis: Fortress Press, 2002).

15. The great hypothesis of Sigmund Mowinckel, often critiqued but never disposed of, has suggested in powerful ways how those myths, in liturgic enactment, functioned in the Jerusalem temple and served the legitimacy of the Jerusalem establishment. See the positive critical response of J. J. M. Roberts to the hypothesis and the reconsideration of it by Ben C. Ollenburger, *Zion: The City of the Great King: A Theological Symbol of the Jerusalem Cult* (JSOT Supplement Series 41; Sheffield: Sheffield Academic Press, 1987).

16. Aubrey R. Johnson, *Sacral Kingship in Ancient Israel* (Cardiff: University of Wales Press, 1955).

17. On the "Royal Psalms," see the older but still reliable study of

Keith Crim, *The Royal Psalms* (Richmond: John Knox Press, 1962).

18. On these metaphors for the High God, see Walter Brueggemann, *Theology of the Old Testament*, 233-50, and G. Ernest Wright, *The Old Testament and Theology* (New York: Harper & Row, 1969), 70-150.

19. Prior to their great programmatic studies cited in n. 14, both Albertz and Gerstenberger published quite detailed studies of the religious practices of sub-communities of clans and families in Israel, studies that unfortunately have not been translated into English: Rainer Albertz, *Weltschoepfung und Menschschoepfung: Untersucht bei Deuterojesaja, Hiob, und in den Psalmen* (Stuttgart: Calwer Verlag, 1974); idem., *Persoenliche Froemmigkeit und offizielle Religion: Religionsinterner Pluralismus in Israel und Babylon* (Stuttgart: Calwer Verlag, 1978); Erhard Gerstenberger, *Der bittende Mensch: Bittritual und Klagelied des Einzelnen im Alten Testament* (Neukirchen-Vluyn: Neukirchener Verlag, 1980).

20. Gerstenberger, *Theologies of the Old Testament*, 224-34.

21. See Walter Brueggemann, *Theology of the Old Testament*, 250-61, for a discussion of these metaphors for YHWH that I have termed "images of sustenance and nurture."

22. Gerhard von Rad, *Old Testament Theology I* (San Francisco: Harper and Row, 1962), 334-47.

23. It is of course the case that in these texts "Moses" refers to Paul's contemporary counterparts in Judaism and not to the ancient covenantal traditions.

24. Krister Stendahl, "Paul and the Introspective Conscience of the West," *Paul Among Jews and Gentiles* (Philadelphia: Fortress Press, 1976), 78-96; more generally, see Ernest Sanders, *Paul and Palestinian Judaism* (Philadelphia: Fortress Press, 1977).

25. See Charles S. McCoy and J. Wayne Baker, *Fountainhead of Federalism: Heinrich Bullinger and the Covenant Tradition* (Louisville: Westminster John Knox Press, 1991).

26. Gerhard von Rad, *Old Testament Theology I*, 439, has identified six proverbs in the book of Proverbs that allow for the slippage of divine sovereignty that subverts an overly simple formulation of *quid pro quo*.

27. 2 Samuel 11–12, concerning the conduct of David, portrays the

king who imagined, for a moment, that he was "outside the Torah." Of course the later phrase "cheap grace," devised by Dietrich Bonhoeffer, concerned the church as it imagined an easy form of obedience to the gospel.

28. This old and current temptation fits well the general thesis concerning faith and economics of Max Weber, *Protestant Ethic and the Spirit of Capitalism* (London: Routledge, 2001).

29. This parable is judged to be "non-authentic" in contemporary scholarship. It does, nonetheless, witness powerfully to the critical perspective of the Gospel of Luke.

30. See Gerhard von Rad, *Old Testament Theology I*, 212-19.

31. Gerhard von Rad, *Studies in Deuteronomy*, 37-44.

32. See the choice comment of Serene Jones, "This God Which Is Not One," *Transfigurations: Theology and the French Feminists*, ed. by C. W. Maggie Kem et al. (Minneapolis: Fortress Press, 1993), 141:

And if this God is truly to meet humanity in a relationship of mutuality, then this God must also be respected as incommensurably other, as a sign as well as an actual event of true alterity.

33. See Terence Tilley, *The Evil of Theodicy* (Salem: Wipf and Stock, 2000).

34. On the silence, see Andre Neher, *The Exile of the Word: From the Silence of the Bible to the Silence of Auschwitz* (Philadelphia: Jewish Publication Society of America, 1981).

35. See Samuel Terrien, *The Elusive Presence*.

36. It is the endless temptation of the church to eliminate the elusiveness of God's presence. Current temptations are reflected in so-called "New Age Religion" that surely seduces the contemporary church in some quarters.

37. See Fredrik Lindström, *Suffering and Sin*, 379-80.

38. On the dialectic of "claiming and ceding," see Walter Brueggemann, "Prerequisites for Genuine Obedience," *Calvin Theological Journal* 36 (2001): 34-41.

39. Claus Westermann, *The Praise of God in the Psalms* (Richmond: John Knox Press, 1965).

40. Patrick D. Miller has observed that even the cry of abandonment in verse 1 is addressed to "my God" (oral communication).

41. In the practice of worship, we must not fail to appreciate the powerful constitutive power of speech, especially when it is liturgical speech as a contradiction of the dominant speech of culture that dehumanizes. On the constructive power of speech and the counter-imagination it permits, see Elaine Scarry, *The Body in Pain: The Making and the Unmaking of the World* (Oxford: Oxford University Press, 1987); William T. Cavanaugh, *Torture and Eucharist: Theology, Politics, and the Body of Christ* (Oxford: Blackwell, 1998); and Walter Brueggemann, "Voice as Counter to Violence," *Calvin Theological Journal* 36 (2001), 22-33.

42. Concerning the ongoing generative power of these recitals, see Gerhard von Rad, "The Form-Critical Problem of the Hexateuch," and Walter Brueggemann, *Abiding Astonishment: Psalms, Modernity and the Making of History* (Louisville: Westminster John Knox Press, 1991).

43. It is important to notice and heed the warning of Tod Linafelt, *Surviving Lamentations: Catastrophe, Lament, and Protest in the Afterlife of a Biblical Book* (Chicago: University of Chicago Press, 2000), that this single statement of hope in the book of Lamentations should not be given excessive weight and should not be permitted to override the unrelieved sadness of the whole. As Linafelt notes, this is a special temptation for Christians who are wont not to linger over the loss in the way Jewish pondering of the loss of Jerusalem lingers.

44. In the liturgical recital of Psalm 136, everything in the memory of Israel is said to be an exhibit of YHWH's steadfast love.

45. See Harvey H. Guthrie, *Theology as Thanksgiving*.

46. Isak Denison, *Babette's Feast and Other Anecdotes of Destiny* (Vintage Books; New York: Random House, 1988), 3-48.

Index

CPSIA information can be obtained at www.ICGtesting.com
Printed in the USA
BVOW030739140613

323325BV00001B/30/P